Healing Stones

Sue Phillips

Healing Stones

©1998 Sue Phillips

ISBN 186163 034 4

Room plan by the author
Beech photography by J. Phillips
All other illustrations & photographs by M. Phillips
Cover design by Paul Mason

Published by:

Capall Bann Publishing
Freshfields
Chieveley
Berks
RG20 8TF

Acknowlegements

I would like to acknowledge the help, friendship and wisdom of Anna Franklin who encouraged me to get writing and without whom my horizons would be very much narrower.

I would also like to thank my family, who have supported me with patience and encouragement throughout.

Dedication

This book is dedicated to Morgan Phillips, my lovely and loving man.

Contents

HEALING STONES

SECTION ONE

Why Stones Rather Than Crystals?

Look in any child's collection of favourite things and you will surely find a small rock or pebble. Ask the child why they keep this bit of "rubbish" and you will generally get the reply "I just like it." Many even give their stones pet names. Why should that be? With the vast range of brightly coloured interactive toys available, why should they elect to treasure a small dull inanimate lump? Whilst writing this book, I spoke to many people of all ages about 'pet stones' and guess what I discovered - many children never voluntarily part from their pebbles. Where there has been no intervention by others, many people still have their stones well into adulthood - often reassigned as paperweights or fish tank ornaments. Strange, that.

Perhaps stones are not so inanimate as they seem.

The truth is, nothing is truly inanimate. The universe is vibrating all the time, every atom of it. It is this vibration that keeps everything together. The actual rate of vibration determines whether an object is hard or soft, liquid, solid or gaseous. Vibration even governs sound and colour and it is through vibration that healing stones work.

For thousands of years, stones and gems have been accorded great ritual significance in most religions and these gems have not always been rare or brilliant stones. Adventurine and carnelian, whilst attractive are classed merely as semi-precious, yet they are amongst the seven most prized gems of the ancient world. Amethyst, once rare and valuable is now relatively common since the discovery of vast supplies in South America. All three are still highly regarded by healers and priests. Fetish stones are simple boulders, which are believed to directly represent deities on earth.

The scientist, Graham Cairns-Smith puts forward an interesting view of crystals as life forms. It is accepted that crystals have geometric forms that can arise spontaneously and then grow and reproduce themselves in a predictable way, whilst retaining individuality, just as any animal form does. Crystalline clays are even closer to living beings, creating complex layers with the ability to evolve in relation to their environment. He suggests that the clay crystals are geological genes, produced by the body of the earth and positioned according to their required function, varying in transparency, porosity and conductivity, but all performing as a kind of crucible in which more complex evolution can take place.

Crystal healing is becoming more and more widely accepted with the corresponding increased pressure on quarries to unearth sufficient suitable gems. Vast tonnages are mined to satisfy the ever-growing demand from collectors and healers alike with little or no regard to the damage being done to subterranean energy fields.

The Earth has been worshipped for aeons as a Goddess in her own right. It was only with the advent of the 'Scientific Age' that the respect traditionally accorded this goddess began to dwindle. This loss of respect has freed humankind from the obligation to care for this mother goddess and we have turned from being her children and become parasites with all that that entails. The idea that the Earth is a living being has again been gaining credence lately, and that we truly are merely an irritating rash on this being is becoming all too apparent. Like any parasite that is not kept in check by the

4

body's natural defences, we are beginning to kill the source of our own life. The entire planet continues to suffer deforestation, over-cultivation, and pollution on an ever-wider scale. We ignore the gifts so abundantly offered to us in favour of the inaccessible, the unobtainable, and the untenable.

Wouldn't it be nice to break that cycle?

This book sets out a method which, whilst working on the same principles as crystal healing, takes only what is freely available on the surface. It shows how to make use of the geological fruits of the earth, the stones and pebbles you can find lying around almost anywhere - in gardens and fields, on hillsides and beaches - or perhaps among your own childhood treasures.

How is it Possible to Heal With Stones?

When we think of our bodies, we tend to think of the dense shell in which we live, the flesh and bones. Contemporary medicine concentrates on treating our ills according to the symptoms that show up there. But there are far subtler aspects to our being than that. We are not made up of a single layer, but of several. You have probably heard of the aura. This is a set of energy fields surrounding the body that can be seen under the right conditions.

The aura has been recorded by a technique called Kirlian photography. These fields are part of us, part of what we are. Their colour and intensity depend on several factors: mood, health, presence of others, spirituality. The aura has an existence semi-independent of the body it surrounds. People who have lost limbs often claim to still have sensations where the limb was, feeling heat, cold and pain. This was put down to nostalgia, until Kirlian photography showed that the shape of the aura still included the missing limb even several years after the loss.

The aura is made up of electromagnetic energy, the same energy emitted from stones and crystals. It is thought that the aura acts as a kind of radio antenna, picking up these crystalline signals. These signals are then processed in the cerebellum, the subconscious rear portion of the brain.

If you find it hard to accept that the brain is capable of such a link, think of a computer. Computers are our attempt to synthesise the human brain. Although they may seem far cleverer than us, with their modern sophisticated programs, they still don't come close to matching our full potential. Most of the brain's activity carries on without our conscious intervention. We don't have to stay awake to keep our hearts beating, or our kidneys functioning - these and countless other tasks are kept going by the unconscious part of our brains. Breathing is slightly different. We can control it to an extent - even choosing not to breathe if we so wish, but breathing is not entirely controlled by voluntary reflexes. As soon as we cease to think about it, whether through sleep, boredom, or unconsciousness, another part of the brain takes over to ensure we don't expire.

Computers have been built to respond to electrical impulses regulated by the atomic vibrations of silicon crystals. The human brain has always been able to do this, within that same area that controls the breathing. We can choose to respond consciously to the vibrations, in which case, the effect will be fairly strong, or we can respond unconsciously. The messages within crystalline forms tend to be very simple and have a straightforward and predictable effect on us - krypton tuning for the cells, so to speak.

Stone circles may have been the prehistoric equivalent to the internet, with magical gems being the personal computers. They are only just beginning to be understood and the more we learn, the more complex their actions seem to be.

Nothing is static. There have been numerous studies into the rate at which different substances vibrate. It is known that the rate and uniformity of vibration will decide whether a substance is liquid, solid or gaseous, with gases being the least regular and crystals the most. This vibrational rate produces the electromagnetic emissions which have been scientifically measured. It is affected by heat and pollution, and this is exploited in the manufacture of computer chips.

Small amounts of pollution are introduced into crystals to make them react in a predictable way, retaining information and programming.

In order to have an effect, the stone to be used must have a vibrational rate similar to that of the person to be healed. It may be hard to think of ourselves as quivering masses of energy, but that is essentially what we are.

Have you ever put your hand on a spin dryer when it is working? You can feel the vibration and if you keep your hand there for a few minutes, it will seem as if your very bones are shaking at the same rate as the spin dryer and this will continue for a short time after you remove your hand. If the machine is standing on a wooden floor, the vibration will probably already have passed along the floorboards to your feet. The vibration of crystalline objects is far more subtle than this, but it works in the same way. The aura picks up the vibration and is affected by it. Because the aura makes up the subtle body, the chief area affected is often the subtlest - the emotions. The slow vibration of a stone with feminine polarity will be calming, whilst the strident note of a masculine stone will be stimulating.

When we are ill, our bodies tend to get 'out of sync' - our lives lose their natural rhythm. A stone programmed to vibrate in sympathy with that natural rhythm will help to restore balance. This is not a quick process and instant cures are not what stone or crystal healing is about, but rather subtle long term re-balancing of the whole person.

Psychometry

Joseph Rodes Buchanan, Dean of Medicine at Covington, Kentucky coined the phrase 'psychometry' [making measurements with the mind] in 1842 to describe people who seemed able to obtain information about a range of objects just by handling them. He noted that around half of his students could identify the contents of a number of securely wrapped packages of similar size and shape, by merely holding them.

William Denton, Professor of Geology at the University of Boston in 1853 employed his sister, Ann in a similar experiment. He asked her to hold a piece of lava from the Kilauea in Hawaii. She described a sea of fire pouring over a precipice and boiling as it poured into the ocean. Realising that this might just be information Ann already had, he took several more rocks from various sources and wrapped them in heavy brown paper. He then mixed up the parcels so completely that even he had no idea which was which. These he presented to his wife, Elizabeth who picked out the one containing the lava without hesitation.

There is strong evidence to suggest that all rocks can act as recorders and their records can be released in the correct hands.

Stefan Ossewiecki was a Polish chemical engineer with a special talent. On thirty-three separate occasions, he was able to describe people from thousands of years ago simply by handling artefacts from archaeological sites. Where this evidence could be checked against known facts, he proved correct in every case, even with hand axes from the Acheulian period around half a million years ago.

In 1941, he was handed a number of prehistoric stone tools. Most were made of flint, a crystalline silicate. One was pure rock crystal. There were various different kinds of items, from harpoon points to scrapers, but all were believed to belong to the Magdalenian culture, thought to be responsible for the cave paintings of Southern France. Ossewiecki described people with broad noses and large heads who buried their dead in urns, used oil lamps, and kept domestic dogs. This did not agree with any of the archaeological evidence, but he remained adamant. Later finds at Zitny in Czechoslovakia and at La Mouth and Chancelade in the Dordogne, France proved him right. His was not a happily ever after story, however as he was murdered at Gestapo headquarters, Warsaw in 1944.

Stones of Power

Rocks, Religion and Legend

The aim of most modern gardeners is to reduce the soil to a fine, stone-free tilth that will produce fine crops or beautiful blooms. Raddles - a kind of soil sieve, have been in use for centuries to remove these obstacles from the pursuit of horticultural perfection. The predominant form of agriculture in Britain was once strip farming. A village or town would have two or three large fields that were divided into strips. Each cottager had one or more of these strips, which he cultivated for food and produce to barter. Stones in the soil were tossed to the margins, as the farmers worked. As time went by, these stones formed ridges separating the strips. Though this kind of farming no longer takes place, the ridges can still be clearly seen on what were once these communal fields.

It is interesting that though these stones were moved aside, they were not actually removed, which would have freed more land for planting. Of course, this could be put down to the basic laziness of human beings, but people were more in tune with the land then. Perhaps they instinctively knew that those stones had a value when kept close by. Since few peasants could read or write; the true reasons were never recorded. The only literate people in the distant past were nobles, who never actually got their hands dirty, and members of the clergy. The veneration of natural objects such as stones, trees or caves was considered heresy, so to mention such ideas to the local priest would have been unwise to say the least.

Stones of the most humble kind have always had a place in the religious and magical beliefs of many cultures. Stones with human or animal form have special significance. At Little Muniton Creek is a stone resembling the head and shoulders of a man bearing antlers which was worshipped as a god. Hunters of the Zuñi tribe would carry stones shaped like animals to bring luck whilst hunting.

In some parts of Scotland, stones shaped like parts of the body were used to treat diseases of those parts they resembled and were named accordingly i.e. eye-stone, leg-stone. The sufferer would wash the affected part and rub it well with the corresponding stone.

In primitive cultures, more in touch with nature than many are today, stones are not seen as an obstacle to productive land, but as helpers. In order to ensure a good yam harvest, New Caledonians performed special ceremonies as they buried yam shaped stones in their plots. Melanesians believed that stones are magically charged according to their shape. The most valuable were shaped like pigs, breadfruit, or yams. Qasavara, mythical opponent of Qat [Melanesian equivalent to Prometheus] fell dead from heaven and like the Egyptian god Ra was turned into a stone upon which those desiring strength in battle subsequently laid sacrifices.

In an age when it was believed that diamonds gave birth to diamonds, stones to stones, a large stone lying with several smaller ones like a sow with piglets was believed to help a barren woman conceive and a stone with circles on would bring money.

People also had their own special stones with a significance that was very personal. From the age of seven, the women of the Kaka tribe from the Cameroons of Africa carried Telembe stones under their tongues. These stones, usually small pieces of quartz, remained permanently in their mouths, even whilst eating and sleeping. They were very precious to their owners and could be exchanged as a sign of friendship. Each woman was familiar with her own stones and could identify them from amongst any number of others, however identical they may appear to be. When a woman knew she was dying, she would distribute her own stones amongst her daughters so that they were passed down through the generations.

There is an interesting legend concerning the origin of frogs in which a woman gave birth to twins and looked for a spring to wash them. She found a well but was driven away by herdsmen so that their cattle could drink. She was met by wolves who led her to a river where she was able to drink and bathe her infants. The woman returned to the well where the herdsmen were bathing. She turned them all into frogs, striking their backs and shoulders with a rough stone to drive them into the water. Since then frogs have lived in marshes and by rivers.

There are several references to rocks and stones in the *Iliad*. Cronos turned people into stones and Zeus petrified a serpent. A stone also gave birth to Agdestis by Zeus.

People of the Andeman Islands in the Bay of Bengal believed in a supreme god who lived in a stone house.

Yacka Torn

To the north east of Western Point in Victoria are some hills said by native peoples to be inhabited by a creature made of stone which no weapon can injure. In an area of these hills called Shaving Point a large rock squats. It is reputed to have once been men who had been fishing and were cooking their catch when a dog approached. They did not feed him and he became angry and called out to them 'You have lots of fish, but give me none!' With that, he turned them into the rock.

In another version of the same legend, the women of the fishing party shouted 'Yacka torn!' [very good] and the dog replied 'Yacka torn!' the party were immediately changed into rocks. A local native named Toolabar claimed that when he was with his father he once heard a dog talk. They quickly ran away before they too became stones.

The Kurnai, an aboriginal tribe from near Wellington, Australia revered a supreme being called Boyma or Baiame who, they explained, dwells in heaven, immovably fixed in a crystal rock with only the upper half of a supernatural body visible. In the same area, is in 1880, a native described his vision of Baiame, which he received when crystal-gazing, as a very great old man with a beard and crystal pillars growing out of his shoulders which prop up the sky.

Hearts of Stone

The Aztec legend of The Creation concerns the god Citlalatonac and goddess Citlalicue who lived in heaven. Citlalicue gave birth to a flint knife, which she flung down to earth. From this sprang 1600 gods. They sent up a hawk to ask the goddess to help them make men to be servants. Citlalicue mocked them, advising them to go to the lord of the homes of the departed and borrow a bone from the dead who dwell with him. The gods took a bone and placed it in a bowl. This they smeared with their own blood. In time, a boy and a girl were born from the bowl and from them came mankind. Two of the gods jumped into a furnace and became the sun and the moon and the two first humans sacrificed themselves to them. They then came back as mystical beings to bring religion to humankind.

Legends about stone women and women turned to stone abound. Cailleach, ancient goddess of the Caldones of the Scottish Highlands was said to be able to turn herself into a stone. There is a standing rock on the upper Missouri that

14

was venerated by the local native tribe who decorated it with animal skins and coloured ribbons. It is said to have been Niobe, a woman whose husband took a second wife and was petrified with grief and on the banks of the Kickapoo river a stone woman was said to dwell in a cave, killing anyone who came near her. The cave is still venerated and treated with caution by many.

The Christian faith accepts that we are formed from the earth. Part of the funeral rite states quite clearly 'Earth to earth, ashes to ashes, dust to dust.' The traditions of the Oneidas and Dacotahs include the claim that they are actually descended from animated stones.

Samoan cuttlefish gods were chased by an Upolu hero who caught them in a net and killed them. They changed into stones and still stand visible in a rocky part of the lagoon on the northern side of Upolu. It is also believed that the first man, Mauke came out of a stone.

Stones played a major part in Iroquois myths. Certain native North American tribes believed human or animal shaped stones were examples of metamorphosis. Among the Aricaras were a girl, her lover, and her dog who ran away from home and were turned to stone when their love did not work out.

The Incas worshipped an emerald in the temple of their supreme deity Pachamac. The Chakchiquels of Guatemala have a creation myth concerning a primeval and animated obsidian stone. There is an Inca legend about a sacred stone that was removed from a mountain. A parrot flew out from it and settled in another stone, which was worshipped from that day forward.

It is said that certain stones near Chincook Point were sea-giants that devoured a man, swallowing him whole. The man's brother used fire to dry up the bay and freed the man who was still alive in the giant's body. The giants were then turned to rocks.

In the Quichua sacred book, *Popol Vuh*, the rising sun changed the lion, serpent, and tiger gods into stone.

The Bushmen of southern Africa have legends about times when they could make stone objects that 'flew over rivers'. Their neighbours, the Hottentots or Khoi-Khoi used sacred quartz knives in sacrifice and circumcisions. In the nineteenth century, a Corporal Maller wrote of great stones on the sides of the paths that the Khoi-Khoi worshipped, pointing upwards and saying: *'Hette hie'* or more likely *'Heitsi Eibib,'* revered god of the Khoi-Khoi. These stones did not always occur naturally but were often erected by the worshippers and daubed with red earth. They performed their religious rites beside cairns of stones that were reputed to be the graves of their god, a healer whose name translates as 'Wounded Knee' and who died and came back many times, hence the numerous graves.

A Bit of the Old Blarney

Most people have heard of the Blarney stone, an inscribed rock slab near the top of one of the walls of the fifteenth century Blarney Castle. Many visitors still come to Blarney, near the city of Cork in Eire to kiss the stone in hopes of gaining the 'gift of the gab' - skill in flattery. Of course, it is not just as simple as walking up to the stone and giving it a swift peck on the north face; one has to actually get under the stone and kiss it from below.

Name That Stone!

The Lia Fail came from the city of La Falias, one of the traditional origins of the legendary Irish folk the Tuatha de Danaan.

The High Kings of Ireland were crowned on this stone. It was said that the stone emitted a roaring sound at the coronation of the rightful king. The Lia Fail was situated in Tara for many generations and a legend grew up that the king of the Irish-Milesians [Celts] would reign wherever this stone rested. It was believed to have been moved to Scotland for the coronation of Fergus the Great at the beginning of the sixth century, where it remained as the famous Stone of Scone until 1297, when Edward I had it moved to England and called it the Stone of Destiny. Up until the coronation of Queen Elizabeth II in 1953, the Stone of Destiny has been used as The Coronation Stone at Westminster Abbey. It was recently returned to Scotland, under the name Stone of Scone amid great celebration.

Whether it is truly the Lia Fail or a copy substituted by the Irish in the sixth century, or even by the Scottish in the thirteenth, may never be proven for sure. The fact remains that this simple stone has been considered a treasure beyond value for many centuries and its importance to all three nations gives no indication of diminishing. Interestingly, the British Royal Family can trace their roots back from the kings of the Milesians. It remains to be seen whether the removal of the stone will affect the fate of the royal family, though their links with Scotland on a personal level are known to be quite strong.

Rest in Pieces

In remote parts of Britain, funerals were difficult to organise, especially if the deceased had dwelt some way from the cemetery. On the road from Dartmoor to Poundsgate, tucked away amid the wild gorse, lies the coffin stone. It is a low granite slab, split in two and carved with very particular graffiti - initials and crosses. When roads across Dartmoor were rough and impassable by wheeled vehicle, coffins were transported by the mourners. The procession was led not by a professional undertaker, but a neighbour, known as the conductor. Six of the mourners would carry the coffin on their shoulders with the rest of the party following on behind in two lines. At a signal from the conductor, the six mourners at the head of the line would speed up and take the place of the coffin bearers. These would then drop back to the end of the line to rest. In this way the bearers were changed regularly and there was often no need to stop until the cortege reached the church. Where the going was particularly rough or steep, the mourners had to pause to rest. The coffin stone was situated in just such a place and as the name suggests, coffins were placed upon it whilst the coffin bearers caught their breath.

It is said that some years ago, the body of a particularly evil person was being transported in this way and when the coffin was placed on the coffin stone, it was struck by lightning, splitting both the coffin and the stone in two.

Runestones

One of the best-known kinds of magical stones are rune stones. Runes are a very ancient script that had great magical significance as well as practical uses. Each letter, or rune, has many meanings. Runic messages were carved on trees and rune stones might be made of wood or clay as well as stone.

In its simplest sense, a rune is a letter which can be put together with other runes to spell words and phrases, in the same way as our modern alphabet. The complete set of runes is known as the Futhark because when laid out in the traditional order, the initial runes in each row correspond to the sounds: 'f', 'u', 'th', 'a', 'r' and 'k'.

In addition, each rune has its own name. The letter E, for example, is called Ehwaz, meaning horse, so that within a word written in runic cypher, there may have been a quite distinct phrase. To further complicate matters, groups of runes related to particular species of tree, such as oak, or birch. The rune's name would indicate its magical meaning. Ehwaz not only stood for the letter E and horse, but also for loyalty! It has two sacred trees: the oak and the ash as well as a magical connection with the herb ragwort.

Divination has always been an important use of runes. Because the runes can be interpreted in so many ways, it is generally considered important to own ones own set, preferably home made. They should be studied and handled frequently until the symbols become completely familiar.

Pieces of jewellery or armour were often inscribed with a rune to protect the wearer or imbue him other with the characteristic of that symbol. Though runes were often used alone they could often be found in combination with other runes as a powerful charm.

Nordic peoples attached great importance to the runes etched on their weapons and they probably saved a great deal of bloodshed. A spear engraved with potent runes and thrown over the heads of the enemy would disempower every man it passed, making him unable to continue the fight! The enemy would run away, or even simply sit down on the spot.

Although their use in battle was important, there has always been another, gentler aspect of the runes. On ancient timbered buildings, the timbers between the brickwork often form intricate patterns. These patterns are not simply the product of artistic inspiration, they are runes, worked into the fabric of the building as a protection! The runic connection would continue indoors, with ordinary everyday objects such as pothooks being made in the form of suitable runes - Eoh being a favourite.

Gentler still is the possibility that runes can also be used to heal.

A powerful healing rune is Ur which represents the now extinct Aurochs, the wild European ox. It brings the stamina to fight off illness and is particularly powerful in combination with Sigil, the rune of the sun, whose power is in the resistance to death and disintegration.

Regenerative powers can be channelled by the rune Ken - which brings enlightenment and illumination

Wyn or Wunjo represents the joy of being in balance with all things. It is the rune of harmony and well being. Its sacred

HEALING RUNES

Letter	U	K	W
Name	Ur	Ken	Wyn/Wunjo
Translation	Ox [Aurochs]	Pine Tree	Joy from being in harmony
Quality	Primal Strength	Torch Knowledge	Prosperity

Letter	Z/Eoh	S	B
Name	Eoh	Sigil	Beorc
Translation	Yew Tree/Bow	Sun	Birch
Quality	Defence	Brightness Victory	Purification Regeneration

Letter	D
Name	Dag
Translation	Day
Quality	Noonday Light

tree is the ash and its herb is flax, the sacred herb from which the goddess Frigg taught mankind to weave linen.

Beorc represents the birch tree. It is primarily a rune with feminine polarity and is invoked in women's magic. It is particularly potent in the treatment of problems peculiar to women. The shape of Beorc is that of the breasts of the earth mother and for this reason it is the birth rune. This is reinforced by its association with the herb, lady's mantle, which is sacred to the mother goddess.

Dag means day. It represents the balance between polarities, particularly dark and light and is a rune of health, light, prosperity and openness. Its function is as a blocking rune and is painted on door frames and window shutters to guard the home from harmful spirits whilst allowing free passage to beneficial ones. Intriguingly, it is also the rune of invisibility. People and objects marked with Dag will not be noticed.

There is nothing very simple about runes. The more I learn, the more there seems remaining to be found out. Before using runes for healing or any other purpose, I strongly recommend you study the subject properly. There are a number of excellent books available.

Fetish Stones and Omphaloi

Fetish Stones

Since the dawn of time, simple boulders have been worshipped as the embodiment of a god on earth. These are termed fetish stones and are almost invariably completely natural. Generally, these stones are worshipped where they lie, though some are moved and legends attach to how the fetish stones came to be at their current location.

The holiest stone of the Hebrews was called Beth-el [dwelling place of deity]. It was kept in the temple of Zion in Jerusalem.

Pilgrims coming to Mecca in search of benediction visit the small black meteor of Ka'aba, the holy stone of Islam. This, they believe is the right hand of god on earth. It is attended by priests, known as the Sons of the Old Woman. To obtain blessing, the stone must be circled widdershins [anticlockwise], against the normal passage of the sun, perhaps because it generates some kind of energy or resonance. In contrast, Buddhist pilgrims walk around their sacred Stupas in a clockwise direction, going with the flow, along the path of least resistance in keeping with their peaceful beliefs.

The ancient British, particularly the Celts were much inclined toward this kind of worship and several laws were passed during the Christianisation of Britain and Europe, outlawing the worship of trees, rivers, wells and stones.

A sacred 'Songline' of the Warramunga tribe of northern Australia was disturbed when the mining town of Tennant Creek removed a 30-ton boulder at a rocky outcrop known as the Devil's Pebbles Aboriginal protests compelled them to replace it in 1981.

Beneath the feet of the statue of Apollo at Delos in ancient Greece lay the simple uncarved fetish stone worshipped long before the statue existed. This unimpressive looking rock was not disregarded when the new statue was carved; rather, the statue was erected to show the true nature of the fetish stone. Elaborate carvings were often made of the gods as civilisations progressed, but the most ancient totems and fetishes, often rude stones, were always considered to be the holiest and the truest earthly manifestation of the deity. In Ach'an Phar' there stood 30 squared stones, each named after a god and worshipped as such.

According to Greek myth, when Rhea married Cronos, father of the gods, Heaven and Earth warned him that his fall would be brought about through his children. In an attempt to avoid his fate, Cronos swallowed them as they were born, causing Rhea great grief. When she came to give birth to Zeus, she substituted a stone for the baby, which she wrapped in swaddling bands. Cronos swallowed it and the child was raised secretly. When Zeus grew up, he forced Cronos to disgorge his children. The stone, swallowed last, was brought out first. Zeus set the stone at Phylo in Delphi [the temple of the womb], where it was revered and covered with wool wrappings on certain feast days.

Another stone cut in a rough pyramid shape was worshipped as Apollo. The Argives worshipped a large stone they called Zeus Kappotas and the Thespians worshipped a stone they called Eros. The list goes on and on. In each case, these sacred stones were very humble rocks indeed - granite, sandstone, or similar.

Perhaps the oldest example of a stone valued in such a way was discovered in 1925 deep inside a limestone cavern inhabited by Australopithecus africanus around three million years ago. It is a piece of red jasperite about the size of a duck egg which is thought to have originated in a streambed twenty miles away. The pebble was still in its natural form, with no evidence of any attempt to carve it, except by the water action of the stream. On one side is a representation of a modern human face. This remained in museum archives until Raymond Dart, a paleontologist with a flair for psychometry came across it whilst working through the store. He looked at the human like face, smiled, and inverted it. Another face appeared of a man with a low brow and heavy chin with a grin so broad that it was obviously a caricature of Australopithecus. We have no way of knowing whether this 'face changing' stone was venerated, but it was clearly treasured.

Omphaloi

Stones marking the centre of the world or omphalos as it is often called [after the Greek for navel] date back at least to the ancient Egyptians. They were generally elliptical in shape and most definitely not of any particularly precious material. The omphalos was the geodetic point where north, south, east, and west met. The centre of Egypt, therefore the world as far as the Old Kingdom was concerned, was at Sakkara and was marked by the holy stone of Sokar, the god of orientation.

The original omphalos no longer exists, but drawings have survived showing it flanked by two birds of prey. In the twelfth dynasty, a stone set in the temple of Amun at Thebes replaced the omphalos at Sakkara, thus changing the geodetic centre of the country.

The ancient Greeks adopted the idea and there is a legend concerning the determination of the centre of the world.

Among his many other titles, Zeus was the grand geometer of the cosmos and in order to measure the world, he sent out two eagles from the Olympian heights, one to the east and the other to the west. They flew in straight lines and met over Delphi, which was therefore designated the centre of the world.

This particular omphalos was originally marked by a baitylos or unworked markstone. It was revered as an emblem of Zeus and remained in place for several centuries, being dressed with ribbons, wool, and branches at festival times. It was later replaced by a more ornate elliptical omphalos which had a gold eagle attached to each side similar to the design of the Theban omphalos. Swags of wool or cloth were carved into the stone as a representation of the decoration of the original stone. The thing I find most interesting about this legend is that it appears to accept that the world is continuous and does not finish at the edges as later civilisations theorised, a remarkable concept for such ancient times.

A similar elliptical markstone exists at Truroe in County Galway, Ireland. The similarities between this and the Delphic omphalos are remarkable. It is the same shape, size and even has the similar spiral patterns over its surface.

There are other omphaloi in Ireland, one at Castlestrange in County Rosscommon is cushion shaped and there are also the stone bases of ancient Pagan pillars at Mullachmast in Kildare and at Killycluggan in County Cavan, both of which were probably originally conical.

Hellige hvide stene or holy white stones are another form of omphalos. They consist of a cylindrical pillar topped with a white stone hemisphere of marble, quartzite or granite.

Although no written records have confirmed this, the phallic shape of these structures indicates that they were probably shrines of Yngvi-Frey, god of regeneration and chief god of the Vanir - the pre-agricultural Norse pantheon.

Clackmannan, Scotland, was once where Pictish kings were inaugurated. By the church stands a large omphalos column marking the centre-point of the land where the spiritual essence is at its height. Similarly in London, the London Stone is reputed to hold the 'luck' and mark the centre of the city. The Blue Stane of St Andrews in Scotland is attributed with the same function. In other areas, blue stones marked the centres of market towns.

Earth Energies and Standing Stones

During megalithic times, it seems that great value was placed on subterranean energy fields. The people living then built structures to enhance and focus these energies where they came close to the surface. Standing stones, huge slabs of common rock, such as sandstone or granite often shaped into long narrow blocks were placed upright in the ground so that the larger portion remained visible. Frequently we find that the top of the stone was carefully sculpted to mimic the landscape from a particular angle. Sometimes notches were cut out of hilltops to line up with corresponding nicks cut into menhirs to allow the sun or moon to be aligned at specific times and seasons.

The remains of ancient alignments of standing stones still exist, mostly in western and northern Europe. They vary from simple pairs of stones, of around $1^{1}/_{2}$ to 16 ft ($^{1}/_{2}$ to 5m) in height and by a few metres apart, to multiple arrangements of 10 or more parallel rows running for a distance of more than 1mile ($1^{1}/_{2}$ km). At Carnac in western France there were originally more than 1,000 stones. Hardly any of them have been dated by radiocarbon, but it is generally assumed that they date from the late Neolithic Period or the Early Bronze Age (3000-1500 BC) and are contemporary with other megaliths in the same area. Alignments in Britain and Brittany have been studied in detail. There are five main types.

Menhírs

The simplest, a standing stone, or MENHIR, often has a flat face that points to a notch or slope on the skyline, aligned to the rising or setting of the Sun or Moon in the most northern or southern position of the year. In areas where the skyline was sometimes 15 miles away or more, these events could be marked very accurately, indicating precisely the passage of the seasons and events such as lunar eclipses. Later menhirs were carved into crosses, or conversely, crosses were carved out of menhirs.

One group of Celts from Northern Britain known as the Picts produced the most intricately carved menhirs and crosses. Designs included ancient religious symbols including sickle moons, crosses, sigils and sun discs together with many animals, particularly the bull, bar, horse, deer, fish, snake, hound and eagle.

On later stones these are combined with Christian images, though it should be remembered that the Christian church did not adopt the cross as its symbol until 680 ad and many crosses pre-dated this time. The easy way in which pagan and Christian symbols were combined on ancient stones has led some scholars to believe the Christian symbols were added later. This is doubtful. The so called battle between the early Celtic Christians and British Paganism has little basis in fact, for many of the earliest Church leaders were Druids who had assimilated Christianity into their beliefs with little difficulty. It was not until far later, when the Roman Catholic Church began to gain prominence that the rift between Christian and Pagan began to appear. The break up reached its most extreme point during the witch hunts and continued after the English Civil war when many ancient customs were stamped out by law - even today, the eating of mince pies at Christmas is technically a crime!

Astronomical Alignments

The alignment of an astronomical event in the second type manifests itself either as a pair of standing stones, in the axis of symmetry of a stone circle, or by a menhir standing outside of a stone circle. In certain alignments, for example at Temple Wood in Argyll, a row of stones may be aligned to several astronomical occurrences. The events marked are mostly the rising or setting of the Sun and Moon; at the solstices and equinoxes; but equally, the alignment may be to the rising or setting of a particular star. In Britain there are alignments which have been shown to form a fairly reliable calendar thought to have been in use during the Early Bronze Age and possibly long after. Stones are aligned to sunrises at the equinoxes and on days intermediate between the solstices and equinoxes, which divide the year into 16 parts of between 22 and 24 days.

The most famous of these constructions is Stonehenge in Wiltshire, built over a period of one and a half thousand years, first from eighty slabs of bluestone, which had to be carried 200 miles from the Prescelly Mountains in Wales. Later these were taken down and replaced with sandstone blocks, some of which weighed over twenty-five tons. These slabs, too, were brought from outside the locality. It has been suggested that they were transported on rails using animal fat as lubricant between the stones and the wooden rails, but there are other possibilities.

In America, a desert once held a mystery. Huge boulders were known to shift up to a mile overnight apparently unaided, leaving straight tracks behind them. Various hypotheses were mooted, including extraterrestrial intervention. The truth finally emerged when cameras were set up to film these stones over a period. It turned out to be a combination of high winds and rain. The rain would turn the earth into a sea of slippery mud and the winds would blow the boulders across the surface like pebbles over ice. Perhaps the stones of Stonehenge were moved in a similar manner. We'll never know the truth of it. Nobody really knows how the huge capstones were raised into position, either, but there is no doubt of the skill of the stonemasons who created the socket joints holding them in place. Later, the bluestones were erected inside the circle and stand there still.

There is more than architecture at work here. It is true that Stonehenge appears to have been built with great care to catch the rays of the setting sun and moon on auspicious days, such as midsummer and midwinter, but the type of stone must also have had great significance. It is hard to imagine the difficulties of carrying just one of these huge megaliths a mile or two even in modern times. How much harder then was it for the ancients to transport so many so far? Why would they bother if these stones did not have particular characteristics necessary for the intended function of the circle?

Sandstone has never been regarded as a precious mineral and modern teachings do not imbue it with any special capability, but there is a local tradition that the stones have healing powers that can be transferred to water and used to treat a wide range of ailments.

Perhaps the key is in the actual make up of the mineral. Sandstone contains a form of very pure quartz, which in its crystalline form is a highly respected psychic tool, used in many ways, and particularly valuable in crystal healing. In common with other sedimentary rocks, sandstone is the geological equivalent of instant mashed potato. It is made up of rocks, which were broken down to fine particles by water action during past ages. These particles were carried along with moving water and deposited in layer upon layer where the current slowed. Gradually the lower layers were pressed down by the weight of more sediment piling on top and hardened into new forms of rock. As the sediments built up, the water channels became choked and blocked, and the water found new paths. Movements in the earth's crust over the millennia have pushed these layers up exposing the stratified rocks far above where they were formed.

The stone circles at Avebury are at least as important as that at Stonehenge, and have the distinction of having been scientifically investigated. Mysterious energies have been detected emanating from these megaliths and they are thought to be able to accumulate and transmute earth energy. Many stone circles have been studied by dowsers, who have found very interesting energies at work. Dowsing, also known as divining is a method of looking for information that cannot presently be picked up by other means and is covered later in the book.

Avenues

The third type of alignment can run for several hundred yards ,consisting of straight rows of stones, usually 3 $\frac{1}{4}$ to 6 $\frac{1}{2}$ feet high and a few yards apart. The rows can be single or double and the ends are sometimes closed by a transverse slab. Many run to small stone circles, some even go beyond and do not generally appear to bear much relation to astronomical events, indicating that their purpose was somewhat different.

This type are most plentiful in Western and Northern areas of Britain, particularly Dartmoor where there is a good supply of suitable stone. Avebury henge is classed as type 3 although in this case, the stones form a winding avenue to the henge - possibly processional ways for important religious festivals. The stones at Avebury have been shown to emit measurable energies that fluctuate with the time of the year. I suspect that there is far more to Avebury than anyone has yet discovered.

Parallel Rows

The fourth type seems to be confined to southern Brittany, in France, centred at Carnac and take the form of multiple parallel rows of stones which number in their hundreds. The paths between the stones are rather winding, though this might be explained by the fact that during the past hundred years, they have been much restored with rather less emphasis on accuracy than might be wished. And it is now impossible to be sure of their original position.

It is believed that they were erected in the late Neolithic Period, from 2500 BC to 2000 BC. As usual, the experts have decided that the entire purpose of the site was a great astronomical observatory. Perhaps it might be considered that stones carefully aligned to astronomical events might at such times be charged with natural energies. Those with the knowledge could direct these forces of nature to the benefit of the people and living creatures in the area.

Fan Shaped Arrangements

The final form of alignment consists of fan-shaped arrangements of small stones, usually less than 3 ft [1m] high. These occur in Carnac and also in north-east Scotland. There has been much speculation as to their purpose, but they could have served as a rock calculator to work out the exact time of the solstices or of the maximum and minimum declinations of the Moon, which do not always relate to the moments of rising and setting.

In General

There are more legends about the origins of standing stones than there are stones standing. One of the stone circles in Brittany is said to be a group peasants who danced on a Sunday and were petrified as a punishment, even though they Pre-date Sunday's adoption as a day of rest by rather a long time. The King Stone, outside the Rollright stone circle is said to be a petrified king. Many stone circles have been investigated by dowsers who use ancient techniques of divining to ascertain the kinds of energies being generated by the stones. Some have been more scientific than others about their methods, but those who took the task seriously have tended to come to similar conclusions.

There are energies flowing all around us. We know about radio waves, light waves, and so forth, but the electro-magnetic energies at work in crystalline structures are only just beginning to be recognised. Everything in existence is moving at all times. Atoms are zooming around their molecules in the same way that the planets move around the sun. In some materials, this movement is chaotic. In others, such as stones and crystals, it is very regular. That is why stones are so hard. The less orderly the inner movement of the atoms of a thing, the less solid it is. The quartz crystal has been used to regulate electronic watches for many years now. Its very exact atomic vibration makes it so successful.

Standing stones also vibrate. There are two basic kinds of vibration. They are referred to, as positive and negative, and their natures are very different. Positive vibrations are energising, revitalising, and strengthening. Conversely, negative vibrations are soothing, calming, and healing. We need balance in our lives, and it is balance that is evidenced in megaliths.

Dowsers have detected bands of energy running through each stone, which, if they were visible would look like horizontal stripes. They are in pairs of positive and negative, often seven pairs in each stone. These energy bands are not consistent, but change with the seasons. In some cases, these changes occur very frequently. In his book, *Needles of Stone*, Tom Graves measured the polarities of the Rollright Stone circle in Oxfordshire morning and night for a week. He found

34

significant differences in the stones and in the rate of polarity changes. Some twelve held the same charge for the entire week, but others had individual cycles, which changed from hour to hour. A few actually changed as often as every twenty seconds.

Graves also studied church altars and found that these too held a charge, but in this case, it was constant. The majority of church altars displayed a positive charge, but altars in the Lady Chapel tended to be negative. Positive charges are also known as masculine, and negative charges feminine. Given the strongly masculine influence of the Christian church, we should not be too surprised at his findings.

In the early 1970's a zoologist was using ultrasound equipment to track horseshoe bats. Just before dawn, he heard a strong regular signal, which was emanating from some standing stones nearby. After a thorough search, he concluded that there were no signs of life and that the sounds had actually come from the stones themselves. A group of scientists later formed the dragon Project and took wide-band ultrasonic detectors and Geiger counters to Stone Age sites. They recorded sounds that could not be attributed to anything but the stones and our friends the Rollright Stones emitted signals that varied with the season, reaching a peak at dawn most mornings. Oddly, these signals could not be detected at all inside some stone circles.

There have been several other studies of standing stones and many functions have been attributed to all of the megaliths. It seems that proof can be found for all sorts of activities, from controlling the weather to being direction-finding beacons. Generally, those making the studies have their own pet theories and are keen to disprove the conclusions of others, so that theirs is the only correct analysis. That is a shame, because there seems to be an element of truth in most of them. The solid state chemist to the project, Don Robins, used X-rays to study the patterns within the atomic structure of crystals. He found that each element consisted of a three dimensional framework of atoms, whose arrangement depended on the purity of the element concerned. Impurities are common and these disturb the pattern and electrical balance of the substance, making it unstable and capable of being altered by the environment. This is known as the 'defect state' and allows information to be trapped in the substance as if it were a magnetic tape, or, more intriguingly, DNA, in which minute flaws in the molecules within a DNA strand allow them to record and transmit genetic change. Technology makes use of this principal every day with the silicon chip, which is made with a calculated dose of impurities to turn the crystals into transistors, semiconductors and microchips.

It would make sense for structures which took so much time and effort to build to be capable of providing more than one service - rather like a post office, where you can post a letter, pay your bills, buy an envelope and often do a thousand and one other things. Though we see Stonehenge today as a mysterious circle of huge stones, its appearance may have been quite different in its day. Experts have conjectured that holes around the stones had held the posts of giant 'A' frames used to move the great megaliths into place. Recently though a new stone circle was found, with posts still in place. The newest theory is that what we see now is the 'skeletal' remains of a huge enclosed building constructed from wood or wattle and daub, and that the missing stone of this and other famous circles, were actually omitted to allow for a doorway! So, there we have yet another possibility.

Ley Lines - Energy Lines

There is a consensus among a number of scholars that the way ancient landmarks and monuments seem to line up is not entirely coincidental. Alfred Watkins was one of the first to notice these remarkable alignments, which he described in his book 'The Old Straight Track'. Earthworks, moats, beacon hills, old churches and standing stones seem to mark out straight tracks or leys running for many miles. Watkins' method of defining ley lines was simple. He would study a detailed map of an area and try to find three points running in a straight line. He would then extend this line in either direction, linking up further sites. To qualify, these sites had to be very close to the line drawn between the first three.

Evidence of such ley lines can be seen in many parts of the countryside and are rather too common to be accidental. Much evidence of ancient sites has been lost over the centuries, either deliberately by religious zealots or by neglect. Dartmoor in Devon, however, still has many undisturbed sites and some seven lines have been identified linking hills, cairns, and hut circles, standing stones, and stone crosses. Two lines run from Cudliptown: one to Lustleigh, and another to Prestonbury Castle, each taking in several hut circles, as well as standing stones. Others run between Church Hill Cross and Ter Hill, Great Links Tor and Merrivale, Brandis Cross and a cairn beyond Fordsland Ledge, Drewsteignton and a hut circle near Cawsand Hill, and Beltstone common and King Tor. There have been various theories mooted regarding the reason for these lines. The simplest is possibly the most logical. Most of these landmarks can be seen from a distance. In other words, if you

37

stand at one, you can see the next and it gives a nice simple method of navigating this dangerous terrain. I would be wary about trying to use any of the Dartmoor lines now, however. Things do change and the moor has many treacherous bogs into which many have disappeared.

Another kind of line has also been identified criss-crossing the British countryside. This, though, does not show so clearly on maps. J Havelock Ellis in his book 'Earth Energies' describes how he and others before and after him dowsed standing stones, churches, and other ancient monuments. They found lines of energy running between them that could be shown to have distinct bands of polarity at different heights. Ellis noted that the standing stones in particular tended to emit specifically masculine or feminine energies. He also discovered that small piles of quartz chips occasionally found near such stones had the effect of interrupting these lines, which would then continue at the next point along their route. When investigating the polarity of standing stones, Ellis was able to duplicate the effect. If a man hammers a stone, or throws smaller stones at larger ones, all will become charged with masculine energies. If a woman does the same, the stones will be femininely charged. Clearly, these polarities were of importance when the stones were erected, though it is not easy to know how they were used. It is interesting, though that the altar stones in the Lady chapels of most ancient churches were femininely charged.

This whole subject is made ever more interesting by stone circles. The energies of stones within or close by a circle, are very individual and, in many cases, change frequently, each stone having its own cycle which may cover a few seconds or many months. These energies then link together in complex networks, like the threads of a spider's web, which shift and change according to the interrelation of the individual parts, making an altogether more powerful whole.

The Rollright Stones.

I recently dowsed the Rollright Stones and found all sorts of lines running between the strangely shaped stones. In the middle of the circle, my pendulum was completely still - dead centre as a friend quipped at the time. Perhaps I had a better experience than some. One researcher took an assistant along to the stones and they stood at different points, one inside and the other outside the circle, to try and define points of entry and exit of specific lines. As soon as they started, they suffered severe headaches and were unable to continue. Perhaps the fact that there were two of them standing on a line and linked by a common goal made them more sensitive to the powerful energies involved.

Holeò Stones

Holed stones are quite simply, stones with a hole in them. Some megaliths take this form. The holes are quite natural, formed usually resulting from water action. The stones at the top of granite stacks like those at West Penwith are a good illustration. The hole would have started as a natural hollow, which over the aeons finally wore right through the upper layer.

When the ancients found such a stone, they saw something of great power and holiness [literally]. Holes in the ground were the repository of the feminine earth powers, of Mother Earth. They would remove and erect them edge on at sites fitting to their purpose. They represented the entrance to the womb of the Mother Goddess, a place of birth and rebirth. Often, upright dolmens were placed in careful alignment representing the male and female aspects at festivals and particularly as fertility symbols. Many marriages and betrothals were sealed by couples who would stand on either side of such a stone and hold hands through the hole, whilst exchanging vows.

Of course, the Mother Goddess nurtures and heals her children, so the stones were also used to request healing from Her. They were believed to hold great power, which was not necessarily linked to underground energies and holed stones of manageable size were frequently moved to where their powers were required. Sometimes they were steeped in liquid such as water or ale and this was then used to transfer the energies to the needful.

Holeð Stanðing Stones

Large holed stones such as the Men an Tol, at Maddern in Cornwall, have been much used over the millennia as healers. The Men an Tol is aligned west south west to east north east, although when the central holed stone was set in concrete it appears to have been moved slightly from it's original position. It's alternative name, the crick stone, is derived from the local custom of crawling on all fours nine times through the hole, widdershins [anti clockwise] to cure 'cricks' in the back such as sciatica and lumbago. Sick children were passed through the hole at particular phases of the moon.

The Tolven holed stone at Gweek, was used in a similar way for ritual healing where the sick child was passed through the hole nine times, to and fro, and then placed on a nearby grassy mound to sleep, with a sixpence placed under its head. Babies were passed through a holed stone to ensure a healthy life, or, as in the case of the Men an Tol, babies suffering from consumption [tuberculosis] were passed naked through the hole and then drawn on the grass, again three times widdershins [anti clockwise]. This would symbolise the returning to the womb of the Earth Mother [through the rounded side], to be reborn, naked and clean [being passed from the flatter side] and returned to the earth to allow the disease to be drawn back down to the underworld.

Smaller Holeð Stones

It is possible to find holed stones of all sizes, even pebbles and all represent the same powers. The smallest, known as hag stones could be threaded on a chain or thong and worn. The hole is said to give the stone particular properties, making it suitable for healing.

In Cornwall, small, decorated holed stones were known as adders' beads or adders' stones. These were in much demand as magical amulets, often as fertility charms. For healing and divination, Druids used snake-stones, which they believed had been formed by adders breathing on hazel wands.

Another type of holed stone also existed, ones deliberately fashioned for the practical purpose of weighting spindles. The making of clothing was seen as a magical act. Even now, we speak of spinning or weaving spells. The spindle spins and turns in the spiral dance of feminine magic and twines the thread of life. Spindles were and are simply narrow rods, usually of wood, weighted at the bottom and notched at the top to hold the thread in position during the spinning process. The bottom weight was called a whorl. It was usually a flat disc with a hole in the centre, and could be made of almost anything, including stone. Decorated stone spindle whorls with clear ritual significance have been discovered in Stone Age cave dwellings. The weaver goddess within any society or religion is always associated with magic, so the antiquity of these artefacts is of great significance.

The Celtic weaver goddess was Arianrhod, mistress of the spiral castle of death, initiation, and rebirth, Caer Arianrhod. The shape of the castle represents the spiralling thread. Her spinning wheel is the wheel of the stars, her threads, the threads of life, death, and rebirth. Arianrhod means 'the moon' and also 'silver wheel'. Similarly in Norse culture, Frigg is goddess of settled life. Her distaff and spindle upon which thread is spun are Frigg's magic tools and the traditional symbol of womanhood. Her patterns were marked on the tools of women's handicrafts, sowing grain, spinning, weaving, knitting, basket making, pottery, all winding, spinning actions in contrast to the more direct activities of traditional male crafts. In her cosmic aspect, Frigg is queen of heaven, keeper of silent knowledge. The hammer of Thor represents male power, which uses physical strength and undeviating actions of hammering and throwing.

In times when patriarchal governments attempted to suppress them, it was the female crafts that preserved the inner wisdom teachings of the goddess. Isis was another heavenly patroness of weaving. She also wove magic and could heal, and these ancient spindle whorls may well have had a place in the magical and healing tools of their Neolithic owner.

Holy Hills

Glastonbury Tor

Naturally formed rocks of the largest proportions had their own powers. Glastonbury Tor was reputed to be the site of the legendary Avalon. It is claimed that King Arthur and his queen, Guinevere are buried here and that the mere at Pomparles bridge near Glastonbury is the lake into which the dying king commanded sir Bedevere to toss his sword, Excalibur. The tor at that time was surrounded by floodwater and marshland, making it virtually an island, giving some credence to the legend. The Chalice well, at the foot of the tor was built by the druids from large stones and its red water gives it its other name: Blood Spring. It is claimed that the the holy grail used by Jesus at the last supper and believed to have miraculous powers was carried to Glastonbury and hidden in this well. As 'grail' is said to have derived from the French for 'blood', Blood Spring may have more than one reference.

Legend has it that Joseph of Arimathea landed at Wearyall Hill [Glastonbury Tor] by boat. He leaned on his staff to pray and the staff took root. It grew into the Glastonbury thorn which still flowers twice a year at Christmas and Easter in front of St John's Church and in the grounds of the abbey. It is believed he founded a church here, built of wattle and daub.

The tor itself is a giant spiral maze and at its summit, is the ruin of St Michael's church, which was built to replace an earlier church, destroyed by earthquake. According to Pagan belief this place cannot be Christianised as it is the entrance to Annwn, a kingdom of the Underworld ruled over by Gwyn ap Nudd, lord of the fairies. It is said that in the 6th century, St Collen went through a secret gateway to visit the fairy king where he found himself in a palace surrounded by temptations. In an effort to protect himself, he sprinkled holy water around him and found himself back on the tor alone.

Everest

To most westerners, Everest is the tallest mountain in the world, conquered in 1955 by Sir Edmund Hilary and Sherpa Ten Sing. To the locals, it is known as Como-Lung-Ma [goddess mother of the universe] and Nanda Devi [mother of the Ganges] and its heights are a place of veneration.

T'ai shan

In China, mountains and rivers were considered sacred. T'ai Shan is China's most sacred mountain and the most sacred of the five mountains of Taoism. This is the religion of the outsider and rebel, the alchemist and magician with the accent on the passive, observant side of human nature to bring about harmony. Taoists accept that the earth is a living entity and their holy sites are centres of living energy.

The seven thousand steps leading up to the Temple of the Jade Emperor have been trodden by pilgrims for thousands of years, some even climbed each step on their knees. The Emperor Shun was said to have climbed T'ai Shan to make the great sacrifices to Heaven and Earth almost four thousand years ago. Through the centuries other emperors continued the tradition and in the 11th century, the mountain was pronounced Equal of Heaven and presented with a magical slab of jade in 1736 by the Emperor Chien Lung.

Chartres

The cathedral of Chartres stands on the site of a megalithic dolmen and a well within a mound. The dolmen is simply constructed of two or three unhewn stones, topped by a flat boulder and the resultant chamber, thought to contain a point of power, was tall enough for a man to pass through.

The energies emanating from it changed with the seasons, charging and energising those who came into contact with them and the site was considered holy ground. It was also later revered by the druids, who built a college at Chartres which became an important centre of druidic teaching.

A prophetic vision foretold that a virgin would give birth to a child. In honour of the vision the druids carved an image of this mysterious virgin with the child on her lap from a pear tree and placed it beside the well, close by the power point. The druids called her 'The Virgin Under The Earth' which was later changed to Virgini Pariturae [the virgin who will give birth to a child]. She was revered for hundreds of years until discovered by the first Christians in the third century. By this time the pear wood was blackened with age and the Christians worshipped her as the Black Virgin. The site became known as 'The Druid's Grotto' and when the church was built, it was set in the church crypt. The well became 'The Well of the Strong'. There is no record of a reason for the name, but logic suggests that warriors might come to drink the waters before battle.

The cathedral seems to be an odd mixture of Christian and pagan with a maze on the floor of the nave. Pilgrims enter by the great west door and walk shoeless to this maze where they dance around its spiral path until they reach the centre where the light from three stained glass rose windows will bring about an alchemical charge, transmuting and transforming the pilgrim and refreshing the soul. In the west aisle of the south transept, a large rectangular flagstone is set diagonally in the floor. At midday on the summer solstice, the sun shines through a clear pane in the stained glass window [of St Apollinaire] onto a peg affixed to the flagstone.

Mauna Loa

Among the volcanoes of Hawaii stands Mauna Loa. Many holidaymakers visit the mountain. They are often warned by locals not to pick up any of the small rocks littering the ground, as souvenirs, as theft of her sacred stones will offend the goddess, Pele, who dwells there. Those who take the warning seriously leave in peace. For the less respectful who take the goddess' stones; retribution is swift and harsh. In 1977, Alan Loffert of Buffalo, New York and his family all gathered rocks and took them home. Within a week, his fourteen-year-old son sprained an ankle and tore a cartilage in his knee playing basketball. Soon after, he broke an elbow during a game of hockey. The boy's twelve-year-old brother damaged an eye muscle when he brushed past a branch whilst running through woodland and broke a bone in his left hand at football practise. The third son fractured his arm playing basketball, broke his other wrist in a fall, and was rushed to hospital with appendicitis. Not to be outdone, Loffert's seven-year-old daughter broke two teeth when she fell off a swing and as soon as the dentist had finished repairing the damage, fell and shattered the same teeth again.

After this unprecedented run of bad luck, the children's mother, Dianne Loffert recalled being warned by a Hawaiian about the goddess. The family packed up the stones and posted them to a friend on the island requesting that they be returned to the foot of the peak. The three youngest children suffered no further accidents, but the fourteen-year-old continued to suffer. He gashed his thigh, dislocated his shoulder, and scalded his hand. His parents quizzed him and he admitted that he had kept three of the rocks hidden in his room. These were sent off to join their fellows and peace was restored to the Loffert household.

Compared to some, the Lofferts got off lightly. Allison Raymond of Ontario, Canada also took some rocks from Mauna Loa. Not long after she returned home, her son broke his leg and developed a severe pancreatic disorder, her husband was killed in a car accident and her mother died of cancer. The spell was broken when she returned the stones. Similar stories abound. The Hawaiian National Park Service receives a large number of packages from around the world, mostly of stones that have brought bad luck and these are all returned to the mountain.

SECTION TWO

This section covers methods of using stones and pebbles to heal.

And So We Begin

That stones can heal, I have no doubt. That you can learn to use them for this purpose, I cannot know, but I have faith.

In order to make use of the healing powers of stones, it is necessary to have certain skills. These are not difficult to acquire, you may well have them already.

The two main skills you will need are dowsing and meditation. It is also as well to know how to shield yourself from any negative energies that might come your way. There is no cause for alarm at this suggestion. It is simple common sense, like clipping on a seatbelt when you get into a car, even though you don't actually expect to have a crash.

Dowsing is another word for divining. Most people have seen or heard of water diviners. The classic diviner walks across a field with a forked hazel twig and it starts to twitch when he gets near to underground water courses. What is less obvious to the casual observer, though, is that the hazel twitch is the instrument of the diviner [or dowser]. It does not have any specific powers of its own. Hazel is used for its flexibility and growth form, which gives branches of equal thickness. It could just as easily be a piece of elder or willow of suitable shape and size. I once picked up a green elder branch that had been broken off by children. Holding it like a hazel twitch, it soon began to perform, almost putting my eye out in the process!

Dowsing can also be done using other tools, including a pair of metal rods bent into 'L' shapes. The dowser holds one in each hand loosely in a way reminiscent of a gunfighter with both guns drawn. When water or any other substance being dowsed for is located, the rods cross over. One might say 'X' marks the spot with this method.

My favourite method is with a pendulum. Its swing can give me a great deal of information and it is something I can carry in a pocket most of the time, so it is readily available. It is also extremely easy to improvise a makeshift pendulum.

Meditation is useful to concentrate the mind and psyche on the job in hand. If you can daydream, you can meditate. The instructions later in this book will make it easy.

Defence also has its place. When studying stones and using them to assist the healing process, you will be opening yourself to the unseen powers and energies surrounding you. Healing tends to involve contact with a lot of unbalanced energy and you will very likely find this imbalance affecting your own energies. Psychic self defence is a series of exercises designed to put a barrier between your energy field and that of the person you are helping.

Warning, warning!

I did not give enough consideration to this aspect of healing when I first started out and found myself absorbing the problems of others. I'd never had tinnitus before I helped a lady suffering from this distressing condition, but I did for a good six months afterwards. A colleague had exactly the same experience, so remember: if someone comes to you seeking help for noises in the ears - defend yourself!

Preparing Yourself

In order to do any form of healing, it is helpful to be in a state of harmony. Bathing, or washing your hands under running water will help to avoid bringing any negative energies of your own to the session.

You will often be dealing with people whose own energies may be seriously out of sync, and will need to put up a shield to prevent yourself absorbing this imbalance.

There is also the matter of the psychic vampire. As a healer, you are almost guaranteed to come across at least one. Psychic vampires are not to be confused with the fictional bloodsucking kind - they don't drink blood, and are usually quite happy to sunbathe! They are normal people who have the ability to absorb the kinetic energy of others. Often they come across as pathetic, helpless creatures who cannot manage on their own and need guidance and encouragement at every step. Sometimes they will be 'psychics' able to read the minds of those around them. They do this by punching holes in peoples' auras and drawing off information and energy. The effect psychic vampires have on others will often be quite marked, people around them will visibly slump or sag as they become brighter and more energetic. The funny thing is, very few are aware of what they are doing. It is an entirely unconscious process.

Psychic vampires are naturally drawn to healers where this transfer of energy is voluntary.

Protecting yourself is simple and effective. You may wish to use one of the techniques detailed below, or devise your own. A useful secondary line of defence is to wear a piece of haematite stone. This will form its own shield around you which will be very difficult to penetrate, unless you so wish it.

Psychic Self Defence

Make yourself comfortable. You may wish to sit, stand, or lie. It isn't important, but if sitting or standing, make sure your feet are flat on the floor. You should make sure you keep 'both feet on the ground' throughout any treatment you may give. Thus you will be well grounded or earthed. Harmful energies will be able to pass through you into the earth, rather than becoming trapped within your own energy field. Equally, your own energies cannot be drained away.

This rule applies whatever healing technique you have chosen to use and not just to stone healing. The job of any healer is to channel healing energies to those in need. The energies should come through, not from you. If this point is not heeded, you will soon feel drained and your life force sapped. Do not underestimate the dangers. Some healers not understanding the principles of energy channelling have died unnecessarily young.

There are a number of protective techniques you can employ, some simple, some complex.

The Power of Prayer

Simply say a little prayer to whatever divinity you worship, asking for protection.

White Light
Imagine yourself bathed in a sphere of white light, which allows you to see out, but shields you from all harm. This is very simple, but it works!

Spiral Protection
Visualise white light coming up from the ground in a clockwise direction, to spiral around you up over your head, then down again into the ground. Imagine this light continually spiralling upwards to your head, then back down into the earth, forming a protective field around you.

The Seven Breaths
This is the most potent protection I know. It not only defends, but helps you to be in harmony with the elements. It is easiest to do sitting or standing.

Be aware of your body, of your breathing. Close your eyes if it helps. Breathe in slowly. As you inhale, imagine a white light coming up out of the ground behind you, rising to a point above your head. Hold the breath for a moment, then breath out, visualising the light descending in front of you, to re-enter the ground as you finish exhaling, leaving behind a glowing arc of white light. Pause again before repeating six times more, making seven breaths and seven arcs of white light in all.

On the next inhalation, imagine the white light coming up to your left and rising in the same way as before, to pause above your head and return to earth to your right. Again, pause and repeat a further six times.

Feel these arcs spinning and rotating to form a sphere of moving light, which will shield you from all harm.

Blue Light
Dark blue light can be used in the same way as white light to provide protection. Simply imaging wrapping a dark blue cape around you.

Connecting to the Divine Energies
Once you have created a protective field around yourself, your are ready to make use of the healing energies from above and beneath you. Remember that you are a channel, a kind of aerial to direct the energies for the benefit of others, not a battery. These energies should not be coming from you. To do this is to actually give away your own life force and will ultimately damage your health. The tree is a traditional symbol of the connection between the various levels of existence; the roots reach into the underworld (not to be confused with hell), the trunk stands in the middle earth where we have our existence, and the branches reach up to the the upper or spiritual realm.

To visulaise yourself as a tree is a helpful way of connecting to these realms. Stand with your feet on the ground and visulaise roots growing down into the earth. It doesn't matter where you are, the rots can grow down from any height, I used to work in a third floor flat, and never experienced any problems. Imagine now, branches growing up from the top of your head. Feel them catching the breeze. Let them connect to the sky.

Breathe in slowly and steadily. As you inhale, let the energy from the earth flow upwards through your roots, up through your body and out of the branches at the top of your head. You are a channel, a connector. The energy is flowing through you. It is not of you.

As you breathe out, let it drop down again into the earth to complete the cycle.

56

Whilst healing, allow the energies to flow through you to the recipient of the healing, keeping the energies flowing smoothly. Maintain firm contact with the ground through your feet.

When the session is complete, visualise a door or curtains closing between you and the recipient, allowing the healing energies to fall back into the earth. Draw back the roots and branches you sent out and close yourself down, drawing the white light closely around you like a cloak and completing the separation between yourself and the person you have been healing. Leave no connection. It will not help them and it may harm you.

Afterwards, go and wash your hands in cold running water to rid your aura of the last traces of any connection, or negative energies.

Dowsing

Unlocking the power of stones requires intuition. A valuable tool for this is dowsing. There are two different basic forms. The first is passive - the use of a pendulum, dowsing rods or hazel twitch to gain information locked up in the subconscious part of the brain, generally believed to be the seat of intuition. The second is active - the use of a dowsing medium - usually a pendulum - to actually affect the activity of energy centres within the body.

Dowsing is rather like riding a bike - easy once you can do it!

For the purpose of simple diagnosis and selecting healing stones, pendulum dowsing is by far the most practical. It has the advantage of being both very portable [try putting dowsing rods in your pocket] and relatively safe - if you've ever got a hazel twitch working properly, you know how easy it is to have it twist up and hit you in the face! A pendulum can swing fairly strongly in the hands of an experienced dowser, but it tends to be easier to dodge.

Once you can dowse, you will find it possible to detect all sorts of things, from underground watercourses to health imbalances. This may be a good point to remind you that though you might be able to pick up a great deal of information by dowsing, only qualified physicians are competent to diagnose specific medical conditions. Don't get above yourself or you will pay the price!

Getting Started Is No Problem!

You've seen dowsers at work and you think you know how it's done. The most important thing is the quality of the pendulum. It must be a perfectly faceted crystal of the clearest quartz, suspended on a silver chain that is exactly six inches long. After all, it is the crystal that moves itself, freed from the pull of gravity by its specially designed chain. So, you spend a goodly sum and take your pendulum and you hold it by the very end of its chain, concentrating on keeping your hand as still as possible, so as not to influence the swing by involuntary muscle movement, and you wait.

And you wait.

And you wait.

You will wait, too; because you have just made some of the most common mistakes of would be dowsers. Firstly, you had no question to ask. Secondly, the involuntary muscle movements you are trying so hard to avoid are tiny signals from the cerebellum. This is the part of the brain that governs the autonomic reflexes. In other words, it keeps your heart ticking and your kidneys working. The cerebellum is the so-called underused portion of the brain that doesn't seem to do much. According to modern teaching, eighty per cent of the brain's capacity is wasted. Well, maybe. Or maybe not. Lastly, there is no doubt that crystal energy exists, it has been measured scientifically, but it is subtle - a natural vibration. The crystal doesn't have invisible arms and legs that it can use to turn its chain into a swing.

So, What Is A Real Dowsing Pendulum?

A pendulum for passive dowsing can be made of almost anything. The two basic components are a thread, hinged rod or chain capable of swinging freely and a weight attached to the bottom. Whether the weight be a button on a length of thread, or a crystal on a silver chain is quite irrelevant. It is merely tool, an extension of yourself, so use whatever you are comfortable with.

For many years I have used a pendulum made of yew wood on a length of string and many people asked where it came from, as they wanted to learn to dowse. The truth was my, yew pendulum might just as well have been made of plastic, or diamonds. The effect would have been exactly the same. I have even dowsed using a Dr Marten boot suspended by one of its laces when someone has telephoned with an urgent question. It made my arm ache, but worked perfectly well.

One comment I would make about your first pendulum: the better balanced it is, the easier you will be able to understand the different swings. Large flat pendants tend to be a bit tricky for the novice, as do hob nail boots, so use something reasonably symmetrical.

For active dowsing, the make-up of the pendulum is more important as it has to have an effect of its own and you will deliberately direct the way it swings. In this case, the most popular is indeed clear crystal, but this is not right or necessary for every occasion.

For the purposes of learning to dowse, the passive method is easiest and safest.

Let's Begin Again

Get a notebook and something to write with. Notes you make now will help with future studies. You are going to learn the art of passive dowsing so take your pendulum, made of whatever you like, and hold it loosely in whichever hand suits you.

To begin with, you might like to get it swinging deliberately. Once it is moving, start asking some questions. It is important at this stage to ask questions to which the answer is a definite yes or a definite no. Either-or questions will cause confusion and frustration, as you won't get a sensible answer.

Some Preliminary Questions To Try

Is my name [say your name]?

Is my name [say someone else's name]?

Am I male?

Am I female?

Keep the pendulum swinging as you ask the questions and watch to see if the direction of the swing changes. To begin with, you may not get much reaction. Persevere, it will come. Many people feel a slight tingling or tickling in the back of the head. This is the intuition switching itself on and is a very good sign. Not everybody has this sensation, often because their own intuitive processes are already active.

When the pendulum starts to move, it should swing one way for the affirmative and another for the negative. This will be individual to you, so you may wish to make a note of it. For me, swinging in a circle means yes and to and fro means no, but this is by no means universal. With some dowsers, the pendulum swings clockwise for yes, anticlockwise for no, and with others it may swing left to right and to and fro. You really do have to take careful note of how it swings for you and you alone. Practice with questions to which you know the answers until you are fairly clear about the way your pendulum will swing and what it means.

Now We Can Be Clever

Positives and negatives of many kinds can be detected with a pendulum. The first kind you already know, but there are also those of polarity and gender. Hold your pendulum over the head of a woman or girl [or friendly female of another specie if you prefer]. It is best if you do this with someone you know - strangers get a bit concerned when things are dangled over them. Allow your pendulum to swing and you will probably notice that the pendulum swing changes, even though you have not asked a question. Now repeat the exercise with a male [of your choice]. This time, the unasked answer will be different! This works on the polarity of the electromagnetic energy in the body. Men and women are 'poles apart', the static electricity moves in opposite directions.

Try it as many times as you like. For thousands of years, women have attempted to determine the sex of their unborn child by suspending a threaded needle or a wedding ring on a piece of cotton over the 'bump' and watching how it moves. Unfortunately, since this is often the only experience they ever have of dowsing, they might not understand the results achieved and may draw the wrong conclusions. At the turn of the century a small device was invented for sexing chicks whilst still in the egg using the same principle. It was basically a glorified pendulum and when tested on a television programme in the nineteen-eighties, was found to work very well.

When you feel confident, you can go onto the next stage and ask questions to which you might not be so sure of the answers.

No Peeking!

Get some obliging soul to fill a container with water stand it among a few similar empty ones while you look away, or make a pot of tea. These should all be covered so that you cannot tell which is which. Hold the pendulum over each container in turn and try to determine which one has water in. The easy way to do this is to say out loud: 'Is there any water in this one?' If you feel silly, just think the question. It should still work.

Now look away again and ask them to put the dishes in a different order. Dowse again as before. Keep this up as long as your assistant's patience lasts. It helps if they want to learn to dowse as well, you can take it in turns. You may be surprised how many times you are right. If you find the pendulum swings on an empty dish, move the dish to another spot and dowse it again. It may be that you have unwittingly divined an underground watercourse.

Try with various other things, foods, personal possessions. Avoid stones at this early stage, the pendulum tends to react slightly differently to crystalline forms. To begin with you might like to hold a sample of the hidden material in your free hand so that your brain has something to go on. Make sure it is the same and not just of a similar kind or you might end up with a little confusion.

The Final Stage

You will now be ready to try asking questions that do not have a clear-cut answer. For example, when dowsing your containers, have your 'assistant' fill one and then empty it. Then when you hold your pendulum over that container and ask 'does this contain water?' you may find that the pendulum swings in a different way. You will then have to ask further questions: 'Has this recently contained water;' or 'is this wet?' I'm sure you can think up other variables on the same theme.

Dowsing The Polarity of Stones

Boy or Girl

Now it is time to look at those stones.

The dowsing of stones works in a similar way, but is a little more interesting. When you hold your pendulum over a pebble, you will find that it is basically either masculine or feminine - remember the man and woman you dowsed. In other words its polarity is either positive or negative, though these terms don't sit too well with me - I'm female and decidedly not negative!

Collect together a number of small stones. They may come from your own garden, or perhaps you have collected some on your travels. Try and have a variety of different kinds to dowse, the results will be more interesting. Sort them into masculine and feminine. Try also dowsing around the perimeter of each stone. You will find that there is a very specific direction to the energy flow of every stone. Mark the results down in your trusty notebook.

Curious Cones

Hold the pendulum at different heights above one stone and watch the swing. This is where things begin to get really fascinating. Every stone has a unique conical energy field that surrounds it in a very specific way. The height and radius of the cone will vary according to the size and type of stone and will be mirrored above and below. If you hold your pendulum above the apex of the upper cone, you will discover that another inverted cone is also present. This holds true for stones of all shapes and sizes, including standing stones and even precious gems. Try it!

Social Stones

Stones react to each other and the situation in which they find themselves.

Take a number of masculine and feminine stones and arrange them on a tray or table. Dowse over and around each stone. Watch how the polarities seem to have changed slightly. There are new energy lines running between the stones, some beneficial, others less so.

Hold your free hand over each stone in turn and try to determine whether it is 'happy' by dowsing, with your pendulum held away from the arrangement. In this case, the pendulum will be swinging in response to your question rather than to the polarity of the stone.

Rearrange them, touching each in turn and asking it whether it wants to be there, moving them all until you have a harmonious arrangement.

Hold your pendulum directly over and around the arrangement of stones and see if you can detect the changes in the individual energy fields of the stones and the new energy lines created by your arrangement.

Naturally, you should be making copious notes - or at least rough sketches of your findings all the time.

Try moving one pebble to a different place and take note of the reaction of it and its fellows. If you are particularly perceptive, you may actually be able to sense the disruption in the energies. When you have finished, always return the stones to their preferred positions, or break up the arrangement and put the stones back where they came from.

Meditation

The type of meditation suggested in this book is called creative visualisation, or pathworkings. They differ from other kinds of meditation in that rather than making your mind a blank, you fill it with images of a journey. As the name suggests, your journey involves going down an imaginary path to places where you can learn to develop spiritually.

Creative visualisations are easy because you don't need to have absolutely ideal conditions to ensure success. They are very similar to daydreams, but the subject of the daydream is chosen consciously for a particular purpose. It may be that you wish to balance the energies within your body, or in a particular place. You may wish to program a stone for a specific purpose, or just get to know your stone. It may be that you just fancy a quick meditation. The reason will vary, the method will not.

By keeping a record of your experiences whilst meditating, you will learn a great deal about yourself. The record will be a private thing. You don't need to show anyone else and don't go using one of those books on the meaning of dreams to interpret what you see during a meditation. The images will be personal to you. Only you can unlock the meaning behind them.

After a meditation, you may like to eat or drink something. This will help to ground you and restore you properly to wakeful consciousness. If you are doing a group meditation, this can be especially pleasant - everyone can contribute a little something. Don't make it a feast, small cakes or crackers are usually sufficient, with a little fruit juice or wine.

How To Do a Creative Visualisation
You can be alone, or you might like to learn as part of a group. This latter has the advantage that one person can talk the others through the visualisation, rather like reading a story out loud. Whichever you decide, find a quiet place where you can avoid being disturbed, and take the telephone off the hook. Avoid wearing constrictive clothing or footwear, but make sure that you will be warm enough for at least the next ten or twenty minutes - nothing spoils the concentration like cold feet!

Either sit, or lie down, whichever is most comfortable. Whether you lie on floorboards or in a soft cosy bed is purely a matter of choice. To begin with, the fewer distractions you have once you have begun the better, though it is not helpful to fall asleep every time you try to meditate.

Relaxation techniques vary from person to person, but this one was taught to me by Anna Franklin and works very well for most people.

First, Learn To Breath!
Breathe in very slowly. Feel the air going into your lungs. Be aware of its quality, its warmth, or coolness. Fill your lungs completely, moving your chest, rather than your shoulders as you inhale.

Hold the breath for a second or two.

Now, breathe out. Don't hurry; take your time. Let your lungs empty themselves completely.

Pause again before taking a second breath.

When you have taken three breaths in this way, you will begin to feel less tense.

Continue to breathe naturally, but be aware of every breath.

Now Relax

As you breathe, start to be aware of your body.

Concentrate on your toes. Wriggle them and then stretch them as straight as you can. Now let them flop. You may need to do this a couple of times before they feel relaxed. Don't worry, there is no rush. If you are prone to cramp, make sure you stretch your toes upwards towards your chin, not downwards.

When you are ready, move onto your feet. In the same way, move them a little and stretch them, tensing them up as much as possible. Again, if you suffer from cramp, turn them up, not down. Now relax them; just let them flop

Tighten your ankles, twist them round a little if you like, then let them relax.

Your calves are next. Tense them up, then let them go floppy.

Do the same with your knees, and then your thighs. Don't rush the process, if you still feel tension in some muscles, repeat the action.

Next, tighten your buttocks [stop sniggering; this is serious]. And relax.

Move on to your lower spine and pelvis. This is not easy, but persevere. Imagine each vertebra in turn, relaxing the spaces in between. Let your spine lengthen slightly. As you work along your body, allow the tension to flow away.

Tense up your upper spine and raise your shoulders as high as you can before letting them drop. Do this two or three times as most tension is locked into this area.

When you are ready, move on to your arms. Tense your upper arms and let them flop. Again, you may need to repeat this a couple of times before they feel truly relaxed.

Do the same with your lower arms and wrists.

Now stretch your fingers. Open your hands like five pointed stars, then let them flop.

Your neck is another area where tension may be chronic, so stretch and turn your head in different directions before letting it go floppy. Snuggle your head into a nice comfortable position.

Screw up your face into a tight grimace, then let go, letting the muscles go lax.

By now, you should be thoroughly relaxed and ready to meditate. In time, you will be able to reach this state of relaxation very quickly, perhaps even within the three preparatory breaths, but there is no real need, unless your life is lived at a gallop and you can only spare five minutes now and again. If this is the case, take some advice from one who has trodden that path and slow down. You will lose far more than you gain if you do not.

When you are ready, begin your meditation. Imagine you are walking down five steps. With each step you are becoming more and more relaxed. By the time you are past the fifth step, you will be fully relaxed. It may help to read through the suggested path workings and record them on audio tape. Remember to leave plenty of pauses between each section. If you are imagining yourself walking along the path, you need to have time to look around you and take note of what you see. Everything has a meaning, which might not be immediately obvious. Try and remember as much as you can and after you have finished, write it down - it may mean quite a lot at some later time.

Enjoy your meditation, but remember you are in control. You won't be asleep, or hypnotised and can stop whenever you like. When you are ready to finish, simply imagine yourself walking back up those five steps, becoming more awake and aware of your surroundings as you ascend. By the time you are at the top step, you will be fully awake, but the feeling of relaxation and general well being may stay with you for some time.

Finding Your Stones

Small Is Beautiful

The important thing to remember in stone and crystal healing is that, as with most things in life, bigger does not always mean better. It is best to apply the homeopathic principle. Properly charged, a small stone can be even more powerful than a large one.

The types of stones and pebbles to be found lying around vary from one region to another, even from one locality to another.

Around Whitby, jet washes up on the beach. At Swanage, you will find amber. On most beaches, you can pick up pebbles of all kinds. I even found a small black stone with a very fine thread of gold running through it whilst paddling in the sea in Wales. Beaches provide happy hunting ground for stone collectors and most households boast at least one stone, brought back as a souvenir of a holiday.

Of course, you don't have to be near a beach to find pebbles.

Commonly, the rounded pebbles found in domestic gardens have been imported as hardcore or gravel during the building of the house. They may also be remnants of former ages when the land was under water. This can be deduced by the rounded appearance of the stones, where they have been worn smooth by water action. The dull grey of granite and flint is often the predominant colour, though white or orange marble and agate often shine out from the rest.

Finding stones is not exactly difficult. Pebbles can be found lying around anywhere and everywhere, from countryside to city street. There is absolutely no shortage. If you own a garden, then I estimate that you have a ninety-nine percent likelihood of having more stones than you will ever need. If you live within striking distance of a park or beach, then the same is true. Most children collect pebbles and shells when they go to the seaside. Often, parents are very deft at returning these to the beach before the end of the holiday, but still many stones find their way inland in little plastic buckets. If this is true of your family, you probably have a collection that is richer than you imagine.

When beginning to look for stones to use for a particular purpose, remember that there is a natural balance of energy in the earth. We tend to be like toddlers let loose in granny's china cabinet when we don't give full consideration to the effects of our actions on nature.

Have a look around your home. See if you have any pebbles lying around that have happy memories. Sit them on your windowsill for a few hours to let them have a little sunlight. Then take each stone in turn and hold it.

Alternatively, go and sit in your garden or local park - or a field if you like. Just relax and open your mind. Look around you. If any pebbles catch your eye, go over and look at them. Stones that are embedded in the ground will be linked in to the subterranean energy field and should not be moved without due consideration for this. If you feel the urge to pick a stone up, do so, making sure you are able to return it to the same place afterward. Any pebbles lying on the surface are usually all right to pick up.

Hold the stone in the palm of your hand and close your eyes, keeping your purpose firmly in mind. How does it feel? Does your hand feel warm or cold? Does it tingle, or feel different in any way? If you drop a stone almost as soon as you pick it up, that one is not for you and should be put back where it came from. Stones may not have brains like yours or mine, but they do seem to know whom they want to be with. Over the years since I began studying stones and crystals, I have seen examples of stones moving from one keeper to another until they came to rest where they were happy.

If you are unsure of the signals you are receiving, or don't think you are actually getting any signals, try dowsing. Questions to ask could be as follows: -

- Does this stone like me
- Does it want to help
- Is it suitable for healing
- Is it suitable for my purpose.
- Does it have another purpose

You could also dowse the polarity of your stone. This is always handy to know.

If you have chosen an area where it is practical, a meditation may help.

Meðitation For Finðing Stones

First, relax. Be aware of your toes. Wriggle them and then stretch them as straight as you can. Now let them flop. If you are prone to cramp, make sure you stretch your toes upwards towards your chin, not downwards.

When you are ready, move onto your feet. In the same way, move them a little and stretch them, tensing them up as much as possible. Again, if you suffer from cramp, turn them up, not down. Now relax them; just let them flop. Now, tighten your ankles, twist them round a little if you like, then let them relax. Your calves are next. Tense them up, then let them go floppy. Do the same with your knees, and then your thighs. Next, tighten your buttocks.

And relax.

Move on to your lower spine and pelvis. Imagine each vertebra in turn, relaxing the spaces in between. Let your spine lengthen slightly. Tense up your upper spine and raise your shoulders as high as you can before letting them drop. Do this two or three times. When you are ready, move on to your arms. Tense your upper arms and let them flop. Again, you may need to repeat this a couple of times before they feel truly relaxed. Do the same with your lower arms and wrists. Now stretch your fingers. Open your hands like five pointed stars, then let them flop.

Relax your neck; stretch and turn your head in different directions before letting it go floppy. Snuggle your head into a nice comfortable position. Screw up your face into a tight grimace, then let go, letting the muscles go lax.

Now, imagine yourself on a path. The path leads to some steps. Look at them. What are they like? Go down the first step and you will feel more relaxed. As you go down the second step you are getting more and more relaxed. Down now to the third step and you are feeling very relaxed. Step down to the fourth step, you are more and more relaxed. Now go down the fifth step. You are completely relaxed and the path stretches ahead of you.

Walk along, taking note of what is around you. The path winds into the distance and you can see the shimmer of water up ahead. Follow the path. Enjoy the journey, take time to look around and at what is at your feet and beside the path.

As you walk on, the sound of waves rolling onto a beach comes to you. The sea is tranquil and shines silver in the light.

You are close to the beach now and you find that the path has become sandy. Dotted here and there are stones and pebbles of all shapes and sizes. Look at them. Does one attract you? Pick it up if you wish. Turn it over in your hand. What is it about this stone that attracts you? If you wish you could take your stone to the edge of the shore and rinse it in the waves.

Hold it up to the light. Hold it high and let the light fall on every part of your stone. Look how the wet stone shines and shimmers. A soft breeze blows across the beach, drying your stone. Be aware of the power of the light, the water, the earth and the air combined in your stone. Feel the power pulsating through it now, into your hands and through your body until you are in harmony with it.

Stay on the beach as long as you wish. Pick up other stones if you want to, or simply stay with the one you have.

76

When you are ready, replace the stone on the beach. You may put it back where you found it, or you may feel it belongs somewhere else.

Turn and go back up the path the way you came. When you reach the first step, you will begin to be aware of your breathing. As you climb the second step, you will be aware of your body and will be more awake. On the third step, be aware of where you are. As you reach the fourth step, you are nearly back to normal, so stretch and be aware of your surroundings. Step up onto the fifth step and open your eyes. You are now fully awake and feeling relaxed and content.

Later, you might like to make a note of what you experienced.

Polarity

In many ways, stones are rather like magnets in that they have a specific polarity. They will be either positively or negatively charged, and this can be easily determined with a simple dowsing exercise.

Hold a pendulum directly over the stone to be tested and watch which way it swings. Some stones will have a masculine charge, others a feminine. Despite what you may read elsewhere, the polarity does not entirely depend upon the clarity of the stone. If you have practised the technique properly, as described earlier in this section, you will have no difficulty in determining the polarity [or gender] of any stone.

If you dowse different points on a stone, you will find that the polarity is not consistent throughout. There will be a distinct direction in which the energy flows. This is important for distance healing, when you may wish to set the stone to emit its energies to someone a long way off. It is also useful to know when setting out stones in an arrangement.

Polarity is important. Different purposes require different energies. Every stone is subtly unique, which is why it is necessary to identify particular stones for particular purposes.

Sometimes, you may find that though the stone seems the right one for a particular job, its polarity is wrong. Fear not - there is a remedy for this.

Gender Bending

If you wish to give a stone a feminine charge, then it will need to be struck several times by a woman. A masculine charge will be produced by the blows being applied by a man. In order to effect a change, it should be struck hard - either with another stone, or by a hammer [though not hard enough to crush it to dust].

The new polarity will be permanent. Stones treated in this way have been known to maintain their charge for thousands of years.

Polarity does not only apply to stones. There are energy lines running up and down our own bodies and through energy centres known as chakras. One set of lines run between our heads and our feet. They are relatively straight when we are healthy, but can tend to get tangled or diverted when all is not well. Stress or illness can cause problems in the energy lines, which in turn can cause further problems with health. Polarity of men and women is different and opposite.

Preparing Your Stones

Many people feel that there is an innate spirituality within all matter, including crystals and stones. The Celts and the Vikings believed that all things contained life force and gave personal names to things that were important to them - one man called his sword 'Legbiter'.

Throughout the world on all continents, the ancients believed that certain rocks were the earthly embodiment of their gods on earth and revered them accordingly. The more they were revered, the more power the rocks acquired. Whether this was because they really did represent a god, or whether the ceremonies and prayers over several centuries built up kinetic energy within the fabric of the rocks is hard to say. The research into standing stones does indicate the presence of great power, which seems to be unique to each individual stone and changes with the energies around it, whether they be magnetic, gravitational or even sonic from chants. All affect the behaviour of the atoms within the stone.

When you have your own set of stones, you will wish them to work to their greatest potential. To do this, there are simple ways of preparing them, which should become a routine.

As stones can pick up energy waves and record them in a similar way to magnetic tape, it is important to know how to clear old 'recordings' in order to input your own. They also have to be charged, rather like a battery, so there will be enough energy for the stone to fulfil its function. The last step in the procedure is to actually 'program' the stone for its new task. Stones are, of course, capable of being programmed more than once, but can only perform one task at a time. They are also fairly easily de-programmed by careless handling. Do not let others touch your stones. Their energies will imprint on the molecules and any programming you may have done will be destroyed at once.

Preparation Routine

Cleansing
Wash your stone in running water. A clean river or stream is best, but taps also provide running water and are adequate for your purposes. As you wash the stone, imagine all the discordant energies flowing out and away into the earth, to combine there with earth energies and bring harmony.

Alternatively, the stone can be immersed in a mild saline solution and left overnight.

Charging
Place it in sun or moonlight to dry. It should be raised above the ground, so that earth energies do not affect the delicate balance of power within it and so that the energy is not absorbed or earthed. The ideal place is on a quiet windowsill. Pendants and strung beads do well when hung from the branches of a bush or tree.

Your decision whether to dry it in sun or moonlight will depend upon the purpose to which it is to be put. The sun will imbue it with its gentle, soothing energies, whereas the moon produces a much more strident radiance giving your stone a very different character. If the stone is left there through day and night, the energies will be well balanced and to begin with, this is simplest.

The phase of the moon will affect the energies entering your stone and account should be taken of this, particularly if you have elected to charge your stone only in moonlight.

Waxing moon represents to pagans the Maiden Goddess whose potential is as yet unfulfilled. Use a white stone for healing related to the waxing moon. This is a good time for starting new projects or relationships and for setting seeds, including seeds of hope. It is a time for all manner of beginnings. Perhaps someone has been suffering from a debilitating illness. The energies of a waxing moon can help to begin to restore their strength. A stone charged in the waxing moon may be helpful for a couple hoping to conceive, though this matter, more than any other is subject to the laws of destiny.

Full moon is a time for positive magic such as blessing, healing and strengthening. It is a time of creativity, so a stone charged at full moon will help where creative energies are needed. The full moon in pagan lore represents the Mother Goddess, her full belly swollen by pregnancy. This is a time of nurturing. Someone struggling in their role of carer or parent may be helped by a stone charged in the full moonlight.

A stone with a reddish hue, or strongly feminine polarity will be particularly powerful.

Stones with a naturally occurring hole are linked to the power of the moon. They are considered to be particularly valuable in healing. They should first be cleansed and prepared as set out below. Charge them in the light of the full moon, and they can then be worn or placed in water the sufferer uses to wash or bathe.

It was once sincerely believed that insanity was directly linked to the lunar cycles, becoming worse at full moon and this is where the term lunatic came from. The birth of the 'scientific age' put paid to such notions, but it is now known that we really are affected by the moon both physically and emotionally. Our bodies are largely made up of water and, like the oceans, this water is affected by the gravitational pull of the moon.

Waning moon is linked to the Goddess in her crone, or wise woman aspect and this is a time for letting the head rule the heart. This is when we should be listening to wise counsel, letting go of bad habits, negative thinking. It is a time for winding down, relinquishing old relationships and situations. This is a time for all manner of cleansing, both your possessions and your relationships. Illnesses linked to negative thought patterns such as grief, depression or stress, especially that which manifests as anger should be treated with stones charged at the waning moon. Black stones work best at this time.

Dark moon is usually overlooked. It is the three days after the waning moon before the new moon reappears in the sky. It is the death time - a time for allowing our old selves, old ideas and beliefs to die to be reshaped and reborn with the new moon. This is a time for looking inward and accepting that no matter what has befallen us, we can begin again. It is a time to halt an illness or thought process which has gone far enough in one direction and turn it round.

Dark moon is a time to prepare for that new beginning and a clear stone is of great value. It is also a time for planning our defences, immunising ourselves against harmful energies. The metallic grey haemetite is a protective stone which has some unusual characteristics making it particularly suitable for charging at this time. Where others will show themselves as either masculine or feminine by the direction of a pendulum's swing, haemetite is one of the very tiny number of minerals which will still a dowsing pendulum held over it. To the uninitiated, it may seem that it has no power. In fact the opposite is true, it has the power of the dark moon.

Programming Your Stone

Before a stone can be used to heal, it has to be told what to do. After all, you wouldn't expect a computer to do anything without its program, would you, and a stone is in many ways a very basic computer. Unfortunately, it doesn't have a keyboard, so other means must be used to input 'data'. This is usually done by powerful thought forms.

Installing The Program
Try this exercise. Take a stone you wish to use for healing. Cleanse it. Charge it on a windowsill exposed to sun and moonlight, making sure no-one else touches it. Take a

relaxing bath, take the phone off the hook and find somewhere warm and quiet where you will be comfortable. Whether you choose to be indoors or out is entirely up to you.

When you are ready, pick up and study the stone, feel it's every facet, every texture. Look into it, at it around it. Now hold it in your cupped hands and sit in a comfortable position. Make sure you will not be disturbed for a few minutes, take the telephone off the hook if necessary.

Relax. Be aware of your toes. Wriggle them and then stretch them as straight as you can. Now let them flop [stretch your toes upwards towards your chin, not downwards].

Move onto your feet. In the same way, move them a little and stretch them, tensing them up as much as possible, turning them up, not down. Now relax them; just let them flop.

Tighten your ankles, twist them round a little if you like, then let them relax.

Your calves are next. Tense them up, then let them go floppy.

Do the same with your knees, and then your thighs and buttocks.

Move on to your lower spine and pelvis. Imagine each vertebra in turn, relaxing the spaces in between. Let your spine lengthen slightly. Tense up your upper spine and raise your shoulders as high as you can before letting them drop. Do this two or three times.

When you are ready, move on to your arms. Tense your upper arms and let them flop. Do the same with your lower arms and wrists. Now stretch your fingers. Open your hands like five pointed stars, then let them flop.

Relax your neck; stretch and turn your head in different directions before letting it go floppy. Snuggle your head into a nice comfortable position. Screw up your face into a tight grimace, then let go, letting the muscles go lax.

Now, feel the stone in your hands. Be aware of it. Breathe in slowly. Hold the breath for a second or two, then let it out slowly. Empty your lungs completely, and pause before drawing air into your lungs again. As you breathe, feel yourself becoming more and more relaxed. Take three further breaths like this, pausing between each transition, until on the third breath, you should be completely relaxed, aware only of the stone.

It is time to give your stone its purpose. Concentrate hard on what you want it to do. Visualise the person you wish to heal. Imagine them as you would expect to see them after the healing has taken place and wish for them the healing energies required to achieve this. Keep it simple - strength for if that person is weak, or tranquillity for the distressed. The simpler the intent, the more chance you have of succeeding.

When you feel the intent is firmly embedded within the fabric of the stone, it is time to take three further breaths. Breathe in deeply, as before, but feeling more alert, be aware of your surroundings, keeping in mind your stone's purpose. With each exhalation of breath, you will feel more and more awake until on third breath, you will be fully alert.

The stone is now programmed for its purpose. This program will last until you wash the stone in running or salt water; or until someone else touches it.

Place the stone back on the windowsill and make sure no one touches it. Alternatively it can be given to the person you wish to heal. As the healing energies are directed toward them, their energies will not affect the programming. They should keep it near them, preferably in a pocket or, in the case of a holed stone, hung around their neck or wrist. Instruct them to place it on a windowsill at night to recharge.

GROUP PROGRAMMING

If you are studying as a group, you may like to include other members of the group in the programming of a healing stone. Of course, this seems to fly in the face of what I have told you about other people touching your stones, but what is life without its little idiosyncrasies?

It can only be done when all members of the group are within the same energy field. If you already meditate as a group, this should not be a problem. You will need to sit in a circle, reasonably close together. Some like to hold hands, others find it unnecessary. I will leave that choice up to you and your friends. Prepare to meditate as usual, though if you usually lie down, you will find sitting up more practical.

> *The person leading the meditation should take the stone, which should already be suitably cleansed and charged.*

> *When the relaxation exercises have been done, the leader of the meditation should encourage the others to sense the power of the circle. Feel the energy moving around the circle. It should be moving clockwise, in the same direction as the sun. As the power rotates around the circle, the individuals blend into one. One single circle.*

> *As the power builds up, the person leading the group should request assistance from the group in preparing a stone for healing. The circumstances should be explained briefly but clearly - for example: we should like to send this stone to a man/woman who has been*

suffering from severe depression. We would like to program it to help him become more positive about his life. Will you help?

If all the group is in accord, then the stone should be passed round clockwise with the flow of energy to each member in turn, who should concentrate on the stone and its purpose.

When all have handled the stone, it should be passed back to the first person who should keep it until it can either be set in a quiet place for distance healing, or given to the recipient.

Finish as you would for a normal meditation, consciously allowing the energy to return to the individuals before breaking up the circle.

Healing Your Space

Have you ever walked into a room and felt uncomfortable, but could not put your finger on precisely what was wrong; and then gone somewhere very similar and felt instantly at ease? Every place has its own atmosphere as individual as a fingerprint.

Energies are flowing around us all the time and although we may not acknowledge them, most of us are aware of their effects. These energies pulsating through the environment, in which we live and work can have a powerful effect on our health. The Chinese art of feng shui is largely concerned with the energy flow in and around buildings and devotees seem to have little doubt that good feng shui will encourage good health and happiness. I don't propose to go into the details of that particular art in this book - I will leave that to the experts, but there are simple ways to create a harmonious atmosphere using suitable stones.

In my own home, the energies used to be all wrong. Though we were not short of friends, few visited. I did not take offence at this. I am not the greatest housekeeper of all time. Some might say I'm really untidy, and I wouldn't disagree with them. The house was not a thing of beauty.

A few years ago, a close friend invited me to the first meeting of a new group which she called the Outer Circle. I had no idea what it was all about, but went along with an open mind. It turned out to be concerned with spiritual development and I learned a great deal - how to meditate, how to see the innate powers of natural objects.

My friend had a small business selling oils, incenses, and crystals at psychic fairs and by mail order. She showed me a basket of small tumble-polished crystals. It was like meeting old friends. I began to study the healing powers of stones and crystals and to build up a small collection of stones of all shapes and sizes.

As I learned more, I began to move my stones into some sort of order. By dowsing, I found out where these stones fitted into my life. In some cases they did not and were given away. Others were there to help certain aspects of my life. Finally, I had several sets of stones all for different purposes. Some had a place in more than one set, but they had their own preferred resting places.

Our main living room had a small triangular boulder of green malachite on the windowsill, a slightly larger chunk of snowflake obsidian on the floor near the door and pebbles and small crystals peppered about the room on bookshelves, windowsills, and tables. Quite a few of the stones sat in boxes and envelopes whilst not in use.

The strange thing is, though, friends began to visit more frequently and would often comment on the lovely homely atmosphere!

The selection of stones for a particular task is always a delicate one. You must first tune in to the vibrations travelling through the space you wish to heal. Is it too tense, or too chaotic? Too strident, or so laid back the atmosphere is actually depressing?

Listen to your instincts. Place stones where they seem to be at home. As often as not, you will find you have a gut feeling about which stones belong where.

If you have trouble working out exactly what is wrong, then dowsing will quite literally point you in the right direction. Create a simple swing chart, dividing the semicircle into segments relating to the various possible causes of disharmony.

Make an accurate, but simple sketch of the room, marking windows, mirrors, furniture and plants. It doesn't matter if you can't draw, simple shapes to denote the objects will suffice.

Place your chart in the space you wish to heal and hold your pendulum directly above the central point at the base of the chart and set it swinging, along the straight edge, asking the question:

What is the main problem with this place?

The pendulum will swing across the relevant answer. Note this down on your layout sketch.

Move your chart to another part of the room and repeat the exercise. It is as well to dowse a number of different areas.

Sometimes the energy disruption is very localised. You may well find that simply moving the furniture, or tidying up is a help.

It is also possible that you will find energy lines running through the area. These lines criss-cross the earth and most cause no problems whatever. There are times, though, particularly where they pass over an underground water table, where these energies become disruptive and need to be checked.

Once you have determined the problem areas, you can begin to select your stones.

Overly tense atmospheres tend to have an abundance of masculine vibrations. The cure is to place a suitably charged feminine stone in the room. If an area is too relaxed, a masculine stone will restore the balance.

If you have detected a disruptive energy line, dowse to find the height of the line. Most energy lines have several layers, some positive, some negative, so the height of the centre of the line is important. When you have determined this, select some small pebbles made from quartz. These may be in the form of sandstone, quartz crystal, or a mixture. Dowse the stones you have to decide which will work best and place these where the line enters your space. Place a few more where the line leaves as well. You may need to use a small table or shelf at the right height, or you could put them in a small bag and hang them on the wall. If you decide on the latter, make sure the bag is not made of paper or acrylic fibres, as both are made from wood [this applies to so-called wood-free paper too].

ROOM PLAN

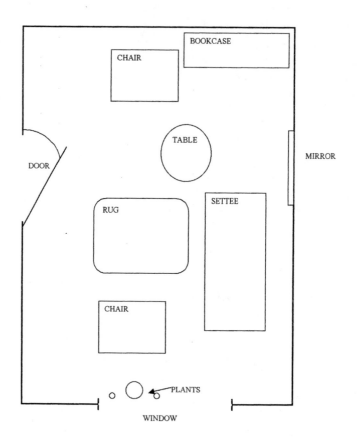

Pathworking For Healing A Room

First, relax. Be aware of your toes. Wriggle them and then stretch them as straight as you can. Now let them flop. If you are prone to cramp, make sure you stretch your toes upwards towards your chin, not downwards.

When you are ready, move onto your feet. In the same way, move them a little and stretch them, tensing them up as much as possible. Again, if you suffer from cramp, turn them up, not down. Now relax them; just let them flop. Now, tighten your ankles, twist them round a little if you like, then let them relax. Your calves are next. Tense them up, then let them go floppy. Do the same with your knees, and then your thighs. Next, tighten your buttocks. And relax.

Move on to your lower spine and pelvis. This is not easy, but persevere. Imagine each vertebra in turn, relaxing the spaces in between. Let your spine lengthen slightly. Tense up your upper spine and raise your shoulders as high as you can before letting them drop. Do this two or three times. When you are ready, move on to your arms. Tense your upper arms and let them flop. Again, you may need to repeat this a couple of times before they feel truly relaxed. Do the same with your lower arms and wrists. Now stretch your fingers. Open your hands like five pointed stars, then let them flop. Relax your neck; stretch and turn your head in different directions before letting it go floppy. Snuggle your head into a nice comfortable position. Screw up your face into a tight grimace, then let go, letting the muscles go lax. Count from one to five slowly. As you count, be aware that you are becoming more and more relaxed so that by the time you get to five, you are completely relaxed.

Imagine yourself in the place you want to heal. Stand in the centre and gradually turn around, looking at every part of the space. Look at the objects present - at the furniture, the windows, the ornaments, pictures and any plants.

As you look you will become aware of lines of energy coursing through the space from all directions. See these lines travelling through some things and bouncing off others. Perhaps some are producing their own. Look at the lines. What are they like? Do they move swiftly, or are they turgid and confused? Perhaps some are moving so quickly that they make you uncomfortable and unsettled.

Look again now at the things in this place and be aware of the effect each has on these energy lines. Is there anything present that is making it hard for the energy to flow smoothly around and through the space? Move things around if you want to, or take them away if they are very disruptive.

Perhaps one of the lines travelling through the space is itself causing problems. If this is the case, find where the line enters and exits. Place a few small pieces of sandstone or quartz at each place. These will act as a shield and you will find that the line vanishes; though, it will continue beyond your space.

When you have done as much as you feel able, count slowly backwards from five to one. As you count you will gradually feel more awake. So that by the time you are at one, you will open your eyes, feeling refreshed.

Make a conscious effort to remember what you have done. Write it down as soon as you can. The next time you are in the place you want to heal, try moving things round as you did in your meditation and see if the atmosphere becomes more comfortable.

Creating Your Swing Chart

Swing charts can be used for many purposes where a simple yes or no answer is insufficient. It can be of value when dowsing problems of a complex nature. Sometimes poor health may have several contributory factors, with maybe only one or two main causes. This is particularly true of allergies. Often a sensitivity to a major allergen such as milk or wheat may actually manifest itself only when other foods are taken. Omitting these secondary foods will give only temporary relief. Only by identifying the primary allergen can a permanent cure be effected.

Mark out a semicircle and divide this into segments, one for each possible answer. See the illustrations for suggested layouts. A good one to begin with is the moon phase chart.

Hold the hand of the person you are intending to help, with the swing chart directly below your pendulum. Set it swinging along the straight line from top to bottom of the chart and ask a question relevant to your chart. The words should be your own and do not need to be spoken aloud, and may be something like:

When should this stone be charged

If the pendulum changes direction and swings over a particular phase of the moon write this down and continue. Set the pendulum swinging along the straight line again and ask if the stone should be charged at any other time. This

98

PERSONAL BALANCE

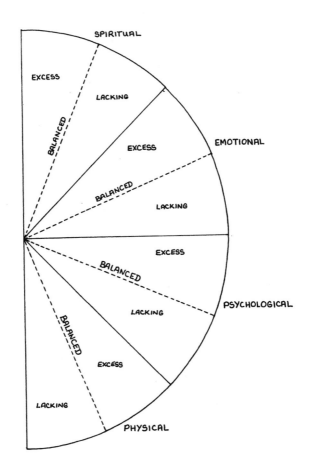

PHASES OF THE MOON

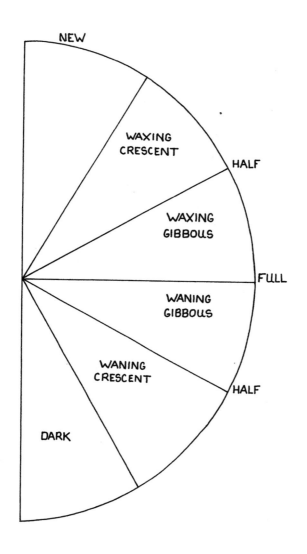

THE CHAKRAS

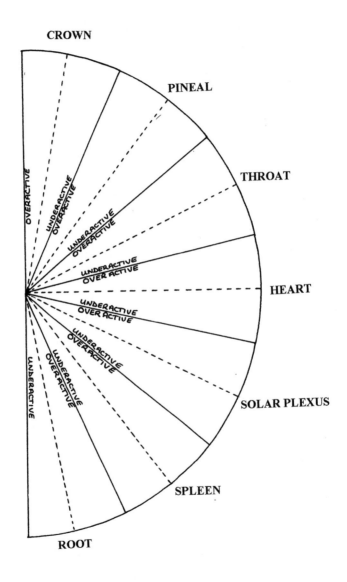

CROWN

PINEAL

THROAT

HEART

SOLAR PLEXUS

SPLEEN

ROOT

OVERACTIVE
UNDERACTIVE
OVERACTIVE
UNDERACTIVE
OVERACTIVE
UNDERACTIVE
OVER ACTIVE
UNDERACTIVE
OVER ACTIVE
UNDERACTIVE
OVERACTIVE
UNDERACTIVE
OVERACTIVE
UNDERACTIVE

may be only one time or it may be a period of several nights, covering more than one phase of the moon.

You should also dowse on whether moonlight, sunlight or both should be used to charge the stone.

The Practicalities of Stone Healing

You have chosen your stones, your room is in harmony, and you are ready to begin to heal. So, what happens next?

We must consider the person you intend to use your new-found skills upon. Stone healing is not like the medicine practised at your local surgery. Treatment is not dictated by the symptoms, but by the needs of the whole person, mind, body, and spirit. It is subtle and has no time limit. A stone charged and programmed today, will not 'cure' a throat infection in seven days. It will regulate and balance the energies within the auric field, which will in turn influence the energies within the body to restore harmony, strengthen the whole person to fight off infections and other harmful influences now, tomorrow and in the future.

Consider the person from every aspect. Select your stone with care. It is well to have several stones charged and ready at any given time. If you are well attuned to them, you should be able to pick out the most suitable by holding your open hand, palm down, above each in turn. Pick out the stone, or stones that feel right. This feeling is a personal thing. You might feel warmth, or tingling, or another sensation entirely. You will know when it happens. If it doesn't, then dowse. Equally, if you are unsure that you have selected appropriately, dowse the stones you have chosen. You may be pleasantly surprised at your intuition.

Masculine stones provide dynamic strength. They will bring feelings of energy, brightness, clarity of thought. They are most effective on short-term conditions, or very severe illnesses where a burst of energy is required to turn the tide. They should not be used for long periods as the effect will be reversed, draining energy away. For distance healing, they should be placed with the positive pole directed towards the recipient.

Feminine stones are more calming. The strength they provide may better be described as fortitude. They will promote restful sleep, soothe frayed nerves, calm hysterics. Overused, they may tend to be somewhat depressing. For distance healing, they should be placed with the negative pole directed towards the recipient.

When you are happy you have the right stones, program them with a single command. No stone can be programmed for two purposes at once. Nor can it be used to treat two people at once, unless they are linked in some way specific to the healing.

The recipient may like to keep the stone with them, in a pocket, or attached to a thong tied around the neck or wrist. Be careful where children are concerned, stones can be swallowed and cause choking, or a cord or thong around the neck can strangle, so sew the stone into something larger, and place it out of the child's reach. So long as it is within a metre or two, it will work effectively and can even be charged to work from your own windowsill for distance healing.

In all cases, as soon as a cure has been effected, or the stone becomes inappropriate due to changes in circumstances, the stone should be 'deprogrammed' by washing and recharging.

Cave Pathworking

First, relax. Be aware of your toes. Wriggle them and then stretch them as straight as you can. Now let them flop. If you are prone to cramp, make sure you stretch your toes upwards towards your chin, not downwards.

When you are ready, move onto your feet. In the same way, move them a little and stretch them, tensing them up as much as possible. Again, if you suffer from cramp, turn them up, not down. Now relax them; just let them flop. Now, tighten your ankles, twist them round a little if you like, then let them relax. Your calves are next. Tense them up, then let them go floppy. Do the same with your knees, and then your thighs. Next, tighten your buttocks. And relax.

Move on to your lower spine and pelvis. This is not easy, but persevere. Imagine each vertebra in turn, relaxing the spaces in between. Let your spine lengthen slightly. Tense up your upper spine and raise your shoulders as high as you can before letting them drop. Do this two or three times. When you are ready, move on to your arms. Tense your upper arms and let them flop. Again, you may need to repeat this a couple of times before they feel truly relaxed. Do the same with your lower arms and wrists.

Now stretch your fingers. Open your hands like five pointed stars, then let them flop. Relax your neck; stretch and turn your head in different directions before letting it go floppy. Snuggle your head into a nice comfortable position. Screw up your face into a tight grimace, then let go, letting the muscles go lax. Count from one to five slowly. As you count, be aware

105

that you are becoming more and more relaxed so that by the time you get to five, you are completely relaxed.

Imagine you are walking along a stony path leading up a hillside. Ahead of you, you see the entrance to a cave. Go through this entrance and look around. To begin with, all seems dark and you hesitate. Gradually your eyes become accustomed to the gloom and you can pick out the direction of the path. Carefully, you make your way down, descending further into heart of the hill.

Now and again, obstacles bar your path and you must choose whether to climb over them, or veer from your path in order to go around them. You become aware that though the path you are travelling is becoming darker, there is a light ahead of you. As you get closer you find that the light is coming from a small chamber in the very centre of the hill.

Stooping low, you squeeze through the tiny entrance and find yourself in a cavern filled light. The walls are made of rocks and they are radiating light and harmony. If you listen, you can even hear the music they make. Stay for a while, bathing in the radiations, letting them heal you and bring harmony to every aspect of your being. When you feel fully restored, thank the rocks within the cave and return the way you came. You may find that the obstacles which appeared in your path on your journey down into the cave now provide handholds to help you climb back to the surface. Count slowly backwards from five to one. As you count you will gradually feel more awake. So that by the time you are at one, you will open your eyes, feeling refreshed.

Recharging Energy Levels

Crystals and stones can help to restore the energy balance of the body by encouraging the energy lines to run in the right directions.

Select two masculine and two feminine crystals. One of each type should be reasonably powerful and the other less so.

Cleanse, charge and program them to rebalance the recipient's, or your own energy field.

Find somewhere to lie down peacefully and place the crystals as follows:

For a Woman

Set the more powerful masculine stone so that its point is directed towards the top of the head.

The more powerful feminine one should be placed at the feet.

The other feminine stone should be placed in the left hand and the lesser masculine one in the right hand.

Ask the person to relax, doing gentle breathing exercises if necessary to help induce calm.

Now, just let them close their eyes and allow the crystals to work.

108

They may feel a slight tugging sensation as the energy lines are pulled straight between the crystals.

They should remain as long as they wish. Generally used in this way, crystals work quite quickly and they may well decide to get up after only a few minutes.

Ensure they take their time, open their eyes and take one or two breaths.

The crystals they are holding should be placed on the floor beside them when they rise [slowly].

As the stones will probably have absorbed some negative vibrations, take them and wash them [a small murmur of thanks wouldn't go amiss at this point].

Set them on a quiet windowsill to recharge ready for next time.

For a Man

Follow the directions above, reversing the order of the crystals, setting a feminine stone at the head and a masculine one at the feet, a masculine stone in the left hand and a feminine stone in the right.

This is the quickest form of crystal healing I know. It works on the basic polarity of the body, which is why the arrangement is different for men and women - electro-magnetically speaking, we really are opposite sexes!

'A funny thing happened on the way to relaxation ....'

Occasionally, you may have unexpected experiences whilst using crystals to balance your energies. Here is one from a student of crystals:

'I was feeling tired and stressed, so as I had to work that night, I decided to recharge my batteries by using crystals. In a quiet room, I lay down with a clear quartz crystal at my head, a pale agate pebble at my feet and a small stone in either hand - feminine pebble in my left and masculine crystal in my right.

Almost as soon as I had completed the basic relaxation, I felt the energies from the stones form a circuit around and through me, restoring me.

As I lay completely relaxed, I had the sensation of my body changing shape, seeming to pull me up and outward, then making me smaller until I was a chicken strutting around, pecking at worms, pulling them out from holes and consuming them. I was aware that these worms were health and personal problems that had needed sorting out for some time. When all the worms were eaten, I felt myself change back to my normal form and after a few more minutes I got up and went out feeling thoroughly cleaned out and refreshed.

I washed the crystals and placed them on my windowsill to bathe in the moonlight.

At the time I was a practising healer and for some time afterwards, saw people's problems as worms and my hen often scratched the soil of their psyche, digging up and devouring them.'

Of course, this experience is exceptional, but it does go to show that crystals properly charged and used do have a profound psychic effect.

Storing Your Stones

There are a number of ways to store stones. If the stone is in use, or if you think you will need a particular stone shortly, then a windowsill, where the sun and moon can shine down on its surface will be ideal. The energies of the sun and moon will keep it charged and powerful. Stones programmed for distance healing should, of course not be touched by others, so keep them out of the reach of children and inquisitive adults.

For longer term storage, or to cloak the energies of a particularly powerful stone, then you might like to use a box made of wood, or better still, paper. Why is paper better: I hear you ask. Remember the childrens' game, Jinx, also known as Stone, Scissors, Paper?

In the game, two children stand facing each other with one hand behind their back and the other in front of them in a fist. The fist is brought up and down as if knocking or hammering. On the third stroke, they must simultaneously make the sign of stone - a fist with the back of the hand uppermost; scissors - the index and middle fingers extended; or paper - the hand held out straight, palm down and fingers together. The rules for scoring are simple, the stronger sign defeats the weaker. Stone blunts scissors; scissors cut paper and paper covers stone.

Why would stone be defeated by being covered by paper? As a child, I used to wonder about that one and found the answer rather unexpectedly. I was for several years a reflexologist and whilst studying, met some people who like myself were interested in stones and crystals. The conversation was easy and relaxed, until all at once I began to feel overwhelmed and jittery. Someone touched me on the shoulder from behind and I jumped. It turned out to be a lady who had just taken a quartz crystal out of an old manilla envelope. She said she used the crystal for healing, letting her patients hold it for a while though she had no idea what effect this might have, only that she thought it might help. The stone was overrun with negative energies from these people and was in dire need of cleansing - holding under running water to allow the energies to rebalance. The reason I had not sensed it before was that the paper envelope had shielded it.

Paper really does cover stone!

And Finally...

The theme of this book is fairly simple. Healing with stones and pebbles is itself fairly simple. It works on the person or place, rather than on a particluar ailment or symptom, so the main requirement is that you select a suitable stone, charge and program it appropriately and then let things happen or not. Destiny will have her way. If you have done your part well, and if the person you wish to heal is destined to be helped, then improvements should follow in their own good time. If not, then nothing you can do will have any effect.

There are a few simple rules to keep in mind at all times whilst using healing stones:

Do-

• Take only the stones you need, and only when there is need.

• Wash stones in running water prior to charging and programming so that there are no confused signals.

• Consider carefully the phase of the moon when charging stones in moonlight.

• Wash the stone after it is no longer needed and consider replacing it where you found it if this is practicable.

• Keep the stones oput of the reach of small children. They do present a choking hazard.

• Have faith in yourself and in the ability of stones to effect a change, even though it may not be quite the change you are expecting.

Don't

• Go digging for stones. There are plenty to choose from on the surface.

• Use a stone without washing it first.

• Assume you can decide the outcome - things sometimes turn out unpredictably, though usually for the best in the long run.

• Let those children get hold of your stones.

• Give up if things start happening right away. Stone healing is a subtle process.

• try to hurry the healing process. It may take many months. On the other hand, it may take just a few minutes, oe even seconds. Every case is a matter of 'wait and see'.

Appendix 1

Classifying Those Rocks

Geologists usually classify the Earth's rocks into three general types: sedimentary, igneous, and metamorphic. Each was formed in a different way.

Sedimentary Rocks

Sedimentary rocks are the product of the earth's climate. They were created when sand, clay, or other materials were deposited by water, wind, or glacial action. The weight of the upper sediment, would drive out water from that below and press the particles together, forming rocks of variable hardness. The most common sedimentary rocks are sandstone and shale.

Shales are composed chiefly of the clay minerals such as kaolinite, mixed with quartz and mica. When calcite or aragonite is present, the shales are called limestones.

The chief mineral of sandstone is quartz, favourite mineral of crystal healers and scryers. If the rock contains significant amounts of feldspar, it is called arkose.

Conglomerates are a subdivision of sedimentary rocks. They are consolidated gravels. Surface sedimentary deposits not yet hardened into rock are termed alluvium. Till, a clay-like alluvium, is thought to have been deposited by glaciers; whereas loess is a fine-grained material that probably started off as windblown dust during the ice ages.

Igneous Rocks

Igneous rocks emerged as volcanic magma, or molten rock from within the Earth's crust. The commonest igneous rock is granite, which is made up of crystals of quartz and feldspar, usually mixed with other minerals. It was formed when magma (molten rock) cooled below the Earth's surface slowly enough to allow small crystals to form. It has been formed in all periods of geological time and commonly occurs in mountain ranges. Igneous rock can also be found in level regions that were mountainous at one time but have since been worn down.

Granite is a very hard stone, but like other rocks it may decay and crumble. Because of its great hardness it is difficult to work and so is an expensive building stone. It is used chiefly as dimension stone for paving blocks, curbing, monuments, and large buildings.

It is one of the most frequently used building stones and is one of the rocks used for standing stones. If a piece of granite is studied under a microscope, it is easy to pick out tiny particles of the separate minerals it is composed of. Thin flat particles of mica reflect light like tiny mirrors, specs of quartz like tiny shards of smoky glass glint amongst the feldspar, which, next to quartz is the most abundant mineral in sandy sediments.

The make up of granite will vary from place to place and the proportions of the minerals will affect the colour. Though the commonest colour is grey, different varieties of feldspar can alter the colour to green, pink or even blue!

Lava is what we see when a volcano erupts. The magma within the Earth escapes through a volcano or fissure at the Earth's surface. There are two common types of lava a dark, heavy variety called basalt and the lighter rhyolite, usually a pale shade of green, red, or grey. Pumice is a porous, frothy form of rhyolite that is produced when molten rock contains gas bubbles.

Tuff is volcanic ash expelled by erupting craters. It often forms a soft rock when deposited in sea or saturated with water and is used for building. Tuff consists of tiny fragments of obsidian or pumice blown into the air during volcanic eruptions. It was tuff that covered Pompeii, suffocating all in its path.

Obsidian is a natural glass that is formed when certain kinds of lava cool so rapidly that the individual minerals do not have time to crystallise. The rock is usually black, but it may be red, brown, or green.

Metamorphic Rocks

Metamorphic rocks have undergone some sort of change. They may have started off as either sedimentary or igneous but have been later modified by heat and pressure or other natural processes to form something quite different.

Gneiss is the most common metamorphic rock. It is derived from either sedimentary rock, such as conglomerate, or igneous rock, such as granite. Gneiss is composed of quartz, feldspar, and mica or hornblende.

Schists are the second most common metamorphic rocks. They were apparently formed when heat and pressure caused the partial recrystallisation of shales. A major type is mica schist. It is composed essentially of quartz, combined usually with muscovite or biotite mica.

Appendix 2

Crystal Systems of Minerals

Mineralogists use six standard crystal forms as a means of classifying and identifying minerals. The crystal systems are based on a series of three or more axes that are considered to exist within every crystal. The forms are distinguished by the length and direction of these axes. These systems are:

Hexagonal
In hexagonal crystals, three axes are of equal length, in the same plane, and equally spaced around the centre; a fourth axis is at right angles to the plane of the other three. A typical form is a six-sided prism. A classic example is quartz.

Isometric
Three axes are of equal length, at right angles to one another in isometric crystals. A typical form is the cubic salt crystal.

Monoclinic
Two axes are at right angles to each other and unequal in length; the third axis, inclined to the plane of the other two, has a different length. A good example of a monoclinic crystal is a prism with its top and base inclined to the sides, like a block distorted sideways. A typical mineral is orthoclase.

Orthorhombic
Three axes are at right angles to each other, each having different lengths. A typical form is a prism having three unequal dimensions. A typical mineral is sulphur.

Tetragonal
Two of the right-angle axes are equal in length; the third is different, either longer or shorter than the other two. A typical form is a square prism, like a section of a square column cut across at an angle. A typical mineral is zircon.

Triclinic
The three axes are unequal in length and inclined to one another. A typical form is a block that has been distorted sideways and lengthways. A typical mineral is albite.

Appendix 3

Attributes of Stones

Some of the stones included in this section are gems, but can be found on the earth's surface and so can validly be used in stone healing.

AGATE

Associated Star sign: Gemini

Technically a semiprecious stone, it is commonly found on beaches and in gardens all over the British isles, South America, the western U.S., and India. Agate is actually a variety of chalcedony composed of chert and fine quartz, with coloured bands. Agate the 'gem' was first found on the banks of the river Achates; and the name evolved from this.

There is a wide variance in the markings to be found on agates, each with its own name and credited with its own particular characteristics - the markings of moss agates, for example, sometimes resemble natural objects and were much prized in the past as amulets. Most agates are naturally greyish and are often artificially coloured by soaking in solutions of sugar or honey and acid or salt solutions and then heated.

Agates can often be found in fields where they were placed in times gone by to assist nature. The ability of agate to attract loyal friends has been exploited by the great and famous over the years, most notably Queen Elizabeth I. Agate improves natural vitality and energy, increasing self confidence. It is good for athletes or those needing to call on instant energy, whether mental or physical. Agate forms a kind of spiritual shield when worn over the solar plexus, helping to deflect the damaging vibrations of others whose fear of the unknown leads to resentment of occultists, but should not be worn by Pisceans or those born under the sign of Virgo. Blue lace agate helps to develop inner peace. Botswana grey agate has a calming and refreshing influence.

AMBER

Associated Star sign: Leo

Amber is a yellow or brownish-yellow translucent fossil resin formed millions of years ago in the Oligocene era. The amber-producing pines grew chiefly on the site of the Baltic and North seas where the land was later submerged. When storms cause rough seas, pieces of amber may be washed up on the shores along seacoasts, particularly around the Baltic and certain British beaches, such as Swanage. Most amber, however, is obtained by mining and this should be avoided for the purposes of healing. Lumps weighing up to 18 pounds (8 kilograms) have been discovered. Small deposits are found in Great Britain, Sicily, Siberia, Greenland, and the United States, but the main source is the Baltic region. It is hard, easily polished, and quickly electrified by friction and is used in jewellery, pipe stems, and so on. When the resin was fresh, soft, and sticky, leaves, flowers, or live insects were occasionally trapped in it. They remained perfectly preserved and may be seen in the amber today.

In ancient Egypt pieces of amber in which the sacred scarab beetles were to be seen were much sought after and these were carved into ritual jewellery. The ancient Phoenicians, Greeks, and Romans also valued amber highly. They believed that it had the ability to cure certain diseases. Amber takes a charge of static electricity when it is rubbed, so the Greeks called it elektron. The word "electricity" is derived from the Greek term.

It is valued as one of the most magical gems, being the only one capable of retaining a magical charge.

Amber of course has legends attached to it. Northern brides wear myrtle as a bridal wreath, in honour of Freya, the love goddess. She married Odur, symbol of the summer sun. One day he went away and Freya was sad without him. Her tears fell into the sea and were transformed into amber. She set out to look for him and crossed many lands. Her tears fell and became the gold found in those places. In the sunny south, she found him beneath the flowering myrtle. They returned home, the flowers bloomed, the grass grew green and the birds sang as they passed.

CAIRNGORM. OR SMOKY QUARTZ

Associated Star sign: Capricorn

Cairngorm, also known as Smoky quartz, or Scots topaz, is one of the most powerful varieties of quartz. Its colour comes from the natural radioactivity in the rocks surrounding the crystal bed. Despite much that has been written about this stone's calming properties, smoky quartz is a very powerful energiser.

The energy levels of this crystal can be quite overpowering, and should be used with caution. It is particularly useful for unblocking the chakras and allowing visions but because of its high vibrational rate can lead to dizziness or more extreme reactions.

Smoky quartz should be packed away in a wooden box or wrapped in paper when not in use as it's powerful energies can disturb the sleep and cause an overcharged atmosphere in the home.

CITRINE

Associated Star sign: Gemini

The citrine, a paler stone of the same variety as smoky quartz is a less powerful stone, and therefore more easily utilised. It is used in place of smoky quartz where a gentler energy is required. Citrine improves poor circulation and helps control emotions.

HAEMATITE

A black crystalline iron; when finely divided, streaked with red, though often dark metallic grey. It is found in England, Norway, Sweden, island of Elba, and Lake Superior region.

Haematite is one of the best protective stones and was rubbed all over the bodies of warriors before battle as it was believed that it would prevent wounds from bleeding. If a pendulum is held over a piece of haematite, it will often cease to swing. This gives an indication of the stone's most particular characteristic. It will protect the wearer by creating a barrier between their aura and the energies being radiated by others and is of particular in cases of psychic attack.

JADE

Associated Star sign: Virgo

Jade is a name applied to jadeite and nephrite. The colour is usually green but a whitish cast occurs occasionally. The stone takes a high polish. Jewellery, cups, and bells are made of it, and poems of Chinese emperors have been carved in priceless jade bowls. In China jade is considered the most precious gem stone as it was believed to engender great purity of thought in its wearer. The ancients called it 'the jewel of the gods' and it is reputed to have great protective powers. It is said to help prevent nightmares. It is a particularly good healing stone because of the combination of its protective and thought purifying influences.

Though jade comes in a number of shades, only the green and lavender varieties are suitable for wearing over extended periods.

JET

Jet Is a black lignite (variety of coal) from coniferous woods with a hardness factor of 3.5, it takes a high polish and is popular for ornaments and costume jewellery. Jet floats in water and is often found washed up on beaches, particularly Whitby in Yorkshire, where articles are available manufactured local lignite alongside imports from Spain. Jet is dedicated to the ancient Greeks to Cybele, goddess of nature and is associated with the planet, Saturn. When carried as an amulet, it will protect a traveller from accident and delays. It is also believed to ward off the evil eye.

Christians believed that jet gave spiritual strength and monks and nuns wore rosaries and bracelets of jet.

Jet is black, the colour of learning. When Queen Victoria went into mourning for her beloved Prince Albert, she dressed in black and wore a great amount of jet jewellery to signify the depth of her grief. This became very popular with her subjects. It is interesting that this fashion coincided with the so-called age of reason, when many new inventions changed life for the people of Britain, and subsequently the world, forever. Jet is also the materialist's stone. It is said that dreams involving jet indicate a materialistic or negative viewpoint. Jet is a good example of the adage: a little may be a blessing, but too much can be a curse.

OBSIDIAN

A smoky natural glass of volcanic formation, abundant in Yellowstone National Park.

Obsidian is used to improve eyesight and promote learning. Snowflake obsidian helps to develop psychic powers. The Chakchiquels of Guatemala have a creation myth concerning a primeval and animated obsidian stone and ritual knives were often made from obsidian.

OPAL

Associated Star signs: Libra, Scorpio

Opal is a species of soft quartz, a non-crystalline silica, often combining several colours and usually opalescent. The play of colour is due to water trapped in minute fissures within the stone. Should this water evaporate, these fissures grow into cracks and the opal can crack or even disintegrate. Opals can be found in muddy areas and appear on the surface in parts of Australia.

Opals are associated with the goddess, Venus. Some believe that opals bring bad luck and for some, this may be the case. To ascertain whether an opal is suitable for an individual, it should be held against the solar plexus. If an unpleasant churning sensation is felt in this area, the opal should not be kept. An opal will not tend to stay with someone they don't like and will either break or be lost should it find itself with the wrong person. The ancients named them the teardrops of the moon and Orientals believe them to be sentient, changing colour according to the emotions of the wearer. It is also said that if the wearer of an opal practises deceit, or abuses the love of another, the vibration of the stone will become negative, bringing misfortune.

The Latin name for opal translates as 'eye-stone' and it was used in the treatment of eye diseases and to sharpen and strengthen the eyesight of the wearer.

QUARTZ

Associated Star sign: Cancer

Quartz is the second most abundant mineral after feldspar. It is formed from the two most common chemicals in the earth's crust, oxygen and silicon. It occurs in nearly all types of rocks and has been found in some rocks collected on the moon and in meteorites. Quartz is also an important constituent of granite. Most sands are weathered fragments of quartz. Sandstone and quartzite are the same materials reformed into rock. Quartz occurs in masses of very fine crystals such as flint, jasper, and agate. It is also found as large crystals. The purest form is clear quartz or rock crystal [from the Greek krystallos]. Gem varieties form when impurities such as lithium, titanium, sodium, and potassium are present and include aventurine, amethyst, chalcedony, citrine, siderite, cat's-eye, and rose, smoky, milky, and rutilated quartz.

Clear quartz is the masculine form of the pure crystal. Its polarity is positive and is used to enhance energy levels, particularly in the treatment of a depleting illness. It is said that the ancient Egyptians developed a method of cauterising a wound with a ball of pure quartz crystal and many healers use rock crystal pendulums both for diagnosis and for healing. The Hottentots or Khoi-Khoi of Africa used quartz knives in sacrifice and circumcisions.

Milky quartz is the feminine aspect of quartz. It has a calming, stabilising influence, excellent for nervous disorders, including insomnia.

Another excellent soporific is the beautiful rose quartz, which if placed near the bed will help to induce restful sleep. It is also useful for treating emotional problems, and kidney disorders, easing the heart of burdens and traumas, leaving it open to love. This is the stone of unconditional love and resentments are replaced by inner peace.

The beautiful amethyst quartz is considered to be an essential part of the healer's collection. The uses of this stone are many and varied and it would require a book to cover them all. It is second to none as a purifier and has the ability to cleanse other crystals of any negative vibrations picked up during healing. Many keep an amethyst cluster for resting crystals between uses.

RUBY

Associated Star sign: Capricorn

Ruby is a form of transparent, red corundum found in clay soil and valued according to shade of colour. Large rubies are often worth more than fine diamonds of the same size. Pigeon-blood (deep carmine-red) rubies, which seldom exceed three carats, are obtained from Myanmar. Darker rubies come from Thailand. Rubies also occur in Sri Lanka, Afghanistan, and North Carolina.

Ruby is said to induce calm, dispel fears, drive away evils of all kinds, inspire confidence and cure liver troubles and blood disorders. The ruby is red, the colour of the root or base chakra and can assist an imbalance here. It should be considered, though, that if a person's astrological chart show any opposition to Saturn, then ruby should not be worn as it may well bring bad luck. It is said that rubies have great effect on relationships, strengthening a good relationship and splitting apart a bad one.